our

Paul Hollywood's
PIES & PUDS

Paul Hollywood's
PIES &
PUDS

Photography by Peter Cassidy

BLOOMSBURY

LONDON · NEW DELHI · NEW YORK · SYDNEY

Note

My baking times in the recipes are for conventional ovens. If you are using
a fan-assisted oven, you will need to lower the oven setting by around 10–15°C.
Ovens vary, so use an oven thermometer to verify the temperature and check
your pie or pudding towards the end of the suggested cooking time.

Introduction

We have a strong culinary tradition in this country, much of it based around the kind of food that fuelled working people: farmers, shepherds, fishermen, labourers, factory workers and so on. Their food may have been frugal and simple but, skilfully made with fresh local ingredients, it could be very good: hearty, delicious and sustaining.

With this book I want to rekindle our affection for that kind of straightforward food, the fare that previous generations thrived on. It's all well and good being able to make a tricky sauce or whip up an elaborate gâteau – those are wonderful culinary skills to have – but there's something about a deep golden home-baked pie or simple steamed pud that warms the cockles of your heart like nothing else. So what you'll find in these pages are simple recipes – unpretentious and comforting – often honed by generations of cooks from particular regions of the country.

I've focused on pies and puddings because I feel these dishes really sum up the strengths of our culinary culture – and because many of my all-time favourite dishes fall into this bracket. Man cannot live by bread alone – not even if the man is me – and a pie can so often give you pretty much an entire meal in a dish.

Not all of these recipes are old-fashioned classics. Some take their inspiration from other cultures – like my spicy chicken and chorizo empanadas and the lovely spinach, feta and pine nut parcels. And some of the sweet options, such as my dark, rich chocolate and prune tart, and irresistible salted caramel and coffee éclairs, are more contemporary. But every recipe is true to the spirit of good, honest, home cooking and at the heart of the book are iconic British dishes such as Yorkshire curd tart, Cumberland rum nicky and my particular take on shepherd's pie.

You'll see that many of the recipes have their roots in the north of England. That's because I'm a northern lad and it's northern cooking that springs to mind when I think of pies and puddings. They remind me of my own youth, growing up in the Wirral. We eat lots of pastry up north and we're very good at making it!

My mum was a great pastry-maker. I remember her one-and-only pie plate, which she would use for all kinds of sweet and savoury pies, every one decorated beautifully with pastry trimmings and baked to a lovely golden brown. As a boy, I would pick sour apples from the tree in our garden, or gather blackberries from round about, and they would all end up in one of Mum's pies. They were the best I've ever eaten: really simple, but so good. She was great at puddings too. The thought of a hot treacle sponge or a bread and butter pudding, waiting for me at dinnertime, got me through many a school day.

Hand-raised pork pies, made with crunchy, hot water crust pastry that broke irresistibly when bitten into, were the stuff of my childhood. And every bakery and chippie where I grew up sold pies and pasties: steak and kidney with a puff pastry top, cheese and potato pie, Cornish pasties with chips – all served drenched with gravy. I was shocked when I moved down south to discover nothing had any sauce!

The dishes in this book do not require great skill or years of baking expertise. Many are the kind of thing our mothers and grandmothers learnt how to cook while they were growing up, and would then be able to turn out for their own families. They may well have made their pastry without even weighing the ingredients, and adapted the filling according to what was cheap and to hand, to create something welcoming and warming out of very little.

Our increasing desire for quick-fix fast food is partly to blame for the waning of this tradition. But I've always believed that time taken cooking a good meal for people you care about is time well spent. There is nothing more therapeutic than putting together a fine suet pudding, nothing more satisfying than the smell of a golden crusted apple pie baking in your oven. And actually, a lot of the time needed to produce a good pie or pudding is not hands-on work time – it's in the chilling of the pastry, the simmering of the stew, or the final baking.

We have also been conditioned to see pastry and sweet puds as unhealthy. But I'd take issue with that. They may not be low in fat, but I would rather eat a fruit-filled pie, topped with pastry made of nothing more than good flour, butter and eggs, than some reduced-calorie, ready-made dessert, full of colouring, corn syrup and preservatives. I'm not suggesting we should all be eating puddings and pasties every night, as people used to do when hard physical labour and huge appetites were the norm, but food like this is a precious part of our culinary heritage and I want to make sure we keep celebrating that.

There are recipes here that will take you all through the year, but you'll find the balance tipped a touch more towards cold weather cooking. For me, pies and puddings are dishes for the autumn and winter, when we all need that little bit of extra central heating. Rain, frost and wind give you the excuse, if you need one, to really ladle on the gravy and be lavish with the custard. Those comforting extras are all part of the experience for me. A pie brimming with savoury juices or a pudding sitting in a moat of hot custard might not be the most glamorous or elegant of dishes, but they are among the most delicious I know. Looks and stylish presentation are not the most important things with these recipes; what matters more is the way they make you feel. This is food that comes from the heart.

Equipment

● ●

It's well worth investing in good-quality baking equipment. You don't need to buy a whole range of cake tins, tart tins and pudding moulds in different sizes – just stock up on a selection of well-made essential items of kit and cooking becomes a breeze, and a pleasure.

Mixers and electric whisks

I'm a great one for doing things by hand but I'd have to say that a mixer or electric whisk can be very useful when making puddings. This is particularly true if you need to beat eggs into a thick moussey state for a light sponge, or if you are whipping egg whites for a meringue. Doing either of these by hand requires a lot of elbow grease! You don't have to splash out too much: you can get a decent hand-held electric whisk for around £20.

Tart tins and baking trays

When baking tarts or double-crust pies (i.e. dishes with a pastry base) you will get a crisper result if you use a metal tin rather than a ceramic dish. To decrease the chance of a soggy bottom even further, it's a good idea to put the tart tin on a preheated baking tray in the oven, which transfers heat directly to the base of the pastry. In all cases, use the best quality metal tins and trays that you can afford: cheap ones are likely to bend and buckle in the oven and can seriously affect your results. The size of tart tins given in the recipes is the diameter or dimensions of the base.

Pie dishes and pudding basins

For pies that have only a pastry top, you can use a ceramic or heatproof glass dish as you don't need to worry about crisping up a pastry base. Choose pie dishes that have a good rim around the edge – at least 2cm wide – so you can anchor the pastry firmly to it.

When steaming puddings, I use ceramic or heatproof glass basins. I also use miniature metal pudding basins and dariole moulds for baking or steaming individual puddings.

Ceramic ramekins and heatproof glass dishes are ideal for baking small custards as they allow the delicate mixture to cook gently.

Cake tins and loaf tins

Again, you need good-quality metal cake tins for the best results. Springform tins are invaluable for turning cakes out easily and stout metal loaf tins are ideal for both cakes and raised pies. I am not a fan of flexible silicone cake moulds: they tend not to hold their shape well, they're not always completely non-stick and they do not conduct heat efficiently.

Rolling pin

I favour a wooden or solid plastic rolling pin. Don't use one with knobs at the end as this shortens the length of the pin, which is unhelpful if you're rolling out a large piece of pastry. I'd go for a not-too-heavy pin which allows you to control the amount of pressure you apply. And of course, make sure your rolling pin is smooth, with no nicks or dents that will transfer to your pastry.

Pie funnel

I often use one of these when I'm making a pie. Placed in the middle of the dish before spooning in the filling and covering with pastry, it supports the pie lid and allows steam to escape, helping to prevent the pastry from becoming soggy.

Knives and cutters

There are a few knives I wouldn't be without: a heavy, sharp cook's knife is ideal for chopping meat and veg for pie fillings; a small, sharp, pointed knife is invaluable for tasks such as trimming the edges off pastry after lining a tin or covering a pie; and a palette knife with a long rounded blade is useful for transferring biscuits and small pies to cooling racks. Sets of plain and fluted cutters are useful for cutting pastry for individual pies and a pastry lattice cutter (available from cookshops) makes light work of creating a lattice pie topping.

Pastry brushes

A pastry brush is a useful tool for glazing pastry and brushing the edges of a pie with water before sealing. I favour the old-fashioned bristle brushes, but modern silicone brushes work well and won't ever shed their bristles.

Baking beans

You can use any type of uncooked, dried beans or rice to line an uncooked pastry case (see page 42), but specially made ceramic beans are nicely heavy and particularly easy to use.

Baking parchment or silicone paper

These are both non-stick, making them ideal for lining tins and baking trays or pastry cases before blind baking. Greaseproof paper is not the same – it does stick, unless you grease it well first.

Cooling rack

This is quite an important piece of equipment because it allows air to circulate underneath a tart, cake or pie as it cools. This not only speeds up the cooling, it also helps to avoid a soggy base.

Ingredients

●●

Many pies and puddings rely on inexpensive, everyday ingredients that you have to hand in your storecupboard or fridge – ready to bring out when the baking urge strikes! My advice is always to buy the best quality you can find.

Flour

It's worth spending a little extra on flour – which is not an expensive item, in any case. In pastries and puddings, it's really the key ingredient so why scrimp on it? There are lots of good-quality flours on the market now, so try out a few different brands to see which you like best.

Most of the flour you'll need for the pastries in this book is plain white flour. This has a protein level between 9 and 11%, which makes it perfect for tender pastry, light sponges and thickened sauces. As with all flours, the quantity of water that plain flour will absorb varies with the brand. So you might find you need to add more or less water to a pastry depending on the brand of flour.

Sometimes I use self-raising flour, which is simply plain flour with raising agents already added. You can convert plain flour to self-raising by stirring in baking powder – allowing about 4 tsp baking powder to 225g flour.

I also use a measure of strong white bread flour in some pastries. Bread flour has a protein level above 12%. This higher level of gluten gives a firmer texture to a dough, which is useful for a robust pastry such as hot water crust, or for pastries that need to hold a high, risen shape such as puff or choux.

Salt

Salt is important in a savoury pastry to stop it tasting dull and bland – a good pinch is all you need for a standard 500g batch. Use a fine-grained table salt that can be easily incorporated into the mix.

Butter

Butter is crucial for flavour in many pastries and puddings, so use the best you can find. I always use an unsalted Normandy butter. As well as a fine flavour, this has a higher melting point than many unsalted butters so it stays firmer for longer as the pastry bakes, and produces a less greasy pastry.

Lard

Lard is rendered down, clarified pork fat. It has a unique, rich flavour and because it is a very pure fat, it forms an impermeable layer in pastry, stopping the pastry from absorbing liquid and thereby keeping it crisp. If you include lard in a shortcrust, you'll get a particularly short, tender and crumbly result, and in a hot water crust pastry, lard gives an incomparable sheen. I like to use a mix of lard and butter – butter for flavour and lard because it lends a unique texture.

Suet

Suet is the fat from around an animal's kidneys. It is very hard and has a high melting point, which gives a unique lightness to pastry. In days gone by, home cooks would buy it from their butcher and chop or grate it by hand. These days, commercially prepared suet is melted down then extruded into little pellets, which are lightly dusted with wheat flour to stop them sticking together. Suet is very easy to use: you can simply stir it straight into your flour, although I often rub it in a little with my fingertips to amalgamate it really well. I usually go for traditional beef suet but, if you prefer, you can use vegetable suet. It will still make good pastry, with a slightly milder flavour and lighter texture.

Sugar

I use lots of different sugars in my baking. Caster sugar is the one I turn to most often: this has fine grains that dissolve easily into a cake mix or a meringue, giving a good, light result. You can use either pure white or golden caster sugar. For sprinkling on the top of sweet pies, I like granulated sugar, which has slightly coarser grains and so gives a lovely crunchy finish.

Soft brown and muscovado sugars are favourite ingredients for puddings and cakes. These contain more of the natural molasses from the sugar cane, which means they have lots of treacly flavour – the darker the sugar, the deeper the flavour.

Icing sugar is very useful for sweetening a pastry dough because it has a similar consistency to the flour and disperses into the mix imperceptibly. You can also use it in a cake or pudding batter if you've run out of caster.

Eggs

These give a rich flavour and colour to pastry, both when used within the mix and when brushed on top as a glaze. The darker and more golden the colour of the yolk, the richer the colour you'll get on your pastry. Of course, eggs are crucial in puddings too: when beaten, they trap air and make for a light mixture, and they are also essential for baked custards, sweet and savoury, where you need the ingredients to set. I use free-range eggs. Generally speaking, the fresher the egg the better – although for meringue, it's helpful to use egg whites that aren't super-fresh, as they are more stable.

Chocolate

I tend to use a good-quality dark chocolate with around 70% cocoa solids for a strong chocolatey flavour that isn't overwhelming. But you can use chocolate with a lower percentage of cocoa if you prefer. Taste the chocolate first: if you enjoy eating it, you'll enjoy what you cook with it.

PASTRY

CLASSIC DOUGHS

TECHNIQUES

PASTRY IS A PRETTY MAGICAL THING. The ingredients couldn't be much more basic or ordinary but, if you bring them together in the right way, the result can absolutely make a dish. We probably all know cooks who have a reputation as fine pastry-makers, and others who say that they're just no good at it. But there's no mystery or secret talent involved. Making excellent pastry is not at all difficult. There are three main things to consider: ingredients, temperature and gluten.

First of all, use good-quality ingredients, and go for brands you know and trust. Don't switch to a new flour, for instance, the first time you make a recipe, because brands can vary, absorbing more or less water. Good-quality pure fats are important too. Cheap butter, for example, usually has an inferior flavour and tends to melt at a lower temperature, making it harder to work with and your pastry more prone to heaviness.

Temperature is crucial with pastry: unless you actually want the fat in the dough to be melted (as in a hot water crust or choux), the cooler your pastry the better. This means the fat is firm enough to work with easily, and stays solid, coating and separating the particles of dough rather than melding with them into a paste. This makes for a light, slightly crumbly pastry rather than a heavy, greasy one. On a hot day, it's even worth chilling your flour for a little while before you begin.

And thirdly, it's important to understand how gluten behaves. Flour contains gluten, a protein which develops into tough, elastic strands when wetted and kneaded. In shortcrust pastries the gluten must be developed only enough to hold the dough together, so a relatively low-gluten flour is used and the dough is handled minimally: too much kneading and rolling will result in a tough, solid pastry. Other pastries have different requirements: puff pastry, for instance, needs a measure of strong flour and a little kneading to give it some structure.

Read my recipes thoroughly and follow them carefully and you will see how the manipulation of a few simple ingredients can lead to an extraordinary range of pastries.

Shortcrust pastry

MAKES ABOUT 450g

●●●●●●●●●●●●●●●●

300g plain flour
Pinch of fine salt
75g cold unsalted butter,
cut into roughly 1cm dice
75g cold lard, cut into
roughly 1cm dice
1 tsp lemon juice (optional)
4–6 tbsp very cold water

The standard proportion for shortcrust pastry is half the weight of fat to flour. Many modern shortcrust recipes use all butter, but I like a bit of lard too. Butter gives a great flavour but the lard creates a particularly short, tender texture. This quantity is sufficient to line and cover a 23cm pie plate.

Put the flour and salt into a large bowl and mix them together. Add the butter and lard dice and toss to coat them in the flour. The fat must be cold when you add it – you want to be able to rub it into the flour without it melting. The fat will then actually coat the grains of flour, helping to keep the pastry nicely crumbly and short.

Now rub the fat into the flour, using your fingertips. Lift your hands above the bowl, rubbing the fat and flour together then letting the crumbs fall back into the bowl. They will trap a little air as they go. Keep going until the mixture looks like fine breadcrumbs. (I prefer to 'rub-in' by hand so I can feel the pastry coming together, but you can use a food processor or a mixer. Process very briefly so you don't overwork the pastry, then tip the pastry 'crumbs' into a bowl, ready to add the water by hand.)

Mix the lemon juice with 4 tbsp water – which, again, should be very cold. The lemon juice isn't essential but it helps to keep the pastry tender because the acid retards the development of the gluten in the flour.

Add the liquid to the rubbed-in mixture and mix in, using one hand; avoid overworking the dough. Add a little more water if necessary, to bring the pastry together.

When the dough just sticks together in clumps, form it into a ball. Knead it very gently on a lightly floured surface to bring it together into a smooth dough. Again, don't overwork it. You can test it by taking a little piece of pastry and rolling it out. If it starts to crack easily, it needs just a touch more kneading to develop the gluten slightly more.

Wrap the pastry in cling film and chill it for about 30 minutes. This firms up the fat and also allows the gluten in the flour to 'relax'. If you leave the pastry in the fridge for much longer than 30 minutes, it may become too firm to roll out easily. Don't worry if this happens, just give it a little time at room temperature to soften slightly.

Adding the diced butter and lard to the flour and salt.

Coating the cubes of butter and lard in the flour.

Starting to rub the fat into the flour, using fingertips and lifting the mixture to aerate it.

Continuing to rub in the fat, breaking it up into smaller pieces.

Step photographs continued overleaf

The latter stage of rubbing-in, when the mixture begins to resemble breadcrumbs.

Adding the liquid to the rubbed-in mixture.

Bringing the pastry together with one hand.

Gathering the cohesive dough into a ball, ready to gently knead.

The smoothly kneaded dough, ready to wrap
and rest in the fridge before rolling out.

Rich shortcrust pastry

MAKES ABOUT 400g
●●●●●●●●●●●●●●●●●

275g plain flour
Pinch of fine salt
1 medium egg
1 tsp lemon juice
2–3 tbsp very cold water
135g cold unsalted butter,
cut into roughly 1cm dice

This is made in a very similar way to the plain shortcrust (page 18), but the addition of egg brings both extra colour and flavour to the pastry. This quantity is sufficient to line and cover a 20cm pie dish.

Put the flour and salt into a large bowl and mix them together. Lightly beat the egg with the lemon juice and 2 tbsp water in a measuring jug with a fork; set aside.

Add the diced butter to the flour and toss the cubes to coat them in the flour. Rub the butter into the flour, using the fingertips. Lift your hands above the bowl, rubbing the fat and flour together then letting the crumbs fall back into the bowl. Keep going until the mixture looks like fine breadcrumbs.

Make a well in the centre of the mixture and pour in the egg mix. Incorporate the liquid into the flour and fat mixture, using one hand; avoid overworking the dough. If it is too dry, add a splash more water.

When the dough just sticks together in clumps, form it into a ball. Knead it very lightly on a lightly floured surface to bring it together into a smooth dough. Again, don't overwork it. You can test it by taking a little bit of pastry and rolling it out. If it starts to crack easily, it needs just a touch more kneading to develop the gluten slightly more.

Wrap the pastry in cling film and leave it in the fridge to chill for about 30 minutes.

Variation: Sweet shortcrust

I often use a sweetened version of this rich shortcrust as the base for an open sweet tart. To make enough to line a 23cm tart tin, follow this method but use 200g plain flour combined with 2 tbsp icing sugar, rub in 100g butter and bind with 1 medium egg beaten with 1 tbsp lemon juice and 2 tbsp water.

Adding the egg to the lemon juice and water.

Rubbing the butter cubes into the flour, using the fingertips.

Adding the liquid to the rubbed-in mixture.

Forming the dough into a ball with the hands once it comes together.

Flaky pastry

MAKES ABOUT 450g
●●●●●●●●●●●●●●●

175g plain flour
Pinch of fine salt
65g cold unsalted butter,
cut into 5mm–1cm dice
65g cold lard, cut into
5mm–1cm dice
1 tsp lemon juice
130ml very cold water

This is a classic pie-topping pastry. Relatively large pieces of fat are trapped in the layers of dough so that when the pastry is baked the fat melts, creating flaky layers, and also releasing steam, which causes the pastry to puff up. This quantity is sufficient to cover 4 individual pies.

Combine the flour and salt in a large bowl. Put the diced butter and lard in a separate bowl, mixing them together loosely.

Take one quarter of the diced mixed fats and rub them into the flour with your fingertips. Combine the lemon juice and water and mix lightly into the flour, using one hand, to form a very soft dough.

Roll out the dough on a well-floured surface to a rectangle, about 10 x 30cm.

Dot the remaining diced fats evenly over the bottom two-thirds of the dough. Now fold the empty top third down and the bottom fat-covered third up over it, as if folding a letter.

Turn the dough 90° and seal the edges by pressing down with your fingers.

Roll out the dough again to a rectangle, about 10 x 30cm. Fold the bottom third up and the top third down over it, envelope-style again. Turn the dough 90° and press the edges down with your fingers. If the pastry is becoming a little soft, wrap it in cling film and chill in the fridge for 20–30 minutes to firm up before continuing.

Repeat the rolling and folding sequence twice more.

Wrap the dough in cling film and leave to chill in the fridge for at least 30 minutes before rolling out and using.

Adding a quarter of the butter and lard to the flour, ready to rub in.

Adding the water and lemon juice to the rubbed-in mixture.

Mixing to a soft dough, using one hand.

Rolling out the dough on a well-floured surface to a rectangle, about 10 x 30cm.
Step photographs continued overleaf

Dotting the remaining fat over the bottom two-thirds of the dough.

Folding the empty top third of the dough down over the middle.

Folding the bottom fat-covered third up over the top.

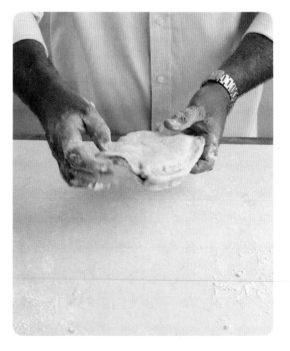

Turning the dough 90° and pressing the edges together to seal.

Rolling out the dough again to a 10 x 30cm rectangle.

Folding the dough into three again to create more layers and pressing the edges to seal.

Rolling out the layered pastry again after chilling to firm it up.

The finished pastry, ready to wrap and chill before rolling out to use.

Puff pastry

MAKES ABOUT 500g
●●●●●●●●●●●●●●●

100g strong white bread flour
100g plain flour
Pinch of fine salt
75–100ml very cold water
165g cold unsalted butter

Puff pastry consists of lots of very thin layers of butter within a dough, created by repeatedly rolling and folding the dough. On baking, the butter melts, making the pastry crisp, and releases steam, puffing the pastry up. The secret to a good puff is to have the dough and butter chilled before you bring them together. If the butter is too soft, it will start to ooze out as you work, and warm dough will become sticky. Chilling the pastry between each 'roll and fold' firms up the butter so you can build up clean, even layers. I use a proportion of high-gluten bread flour to give the pastry the strength it needs to hold its layered structure.

Combine the flours and salt in a bowl. Mix in enough water to form a reasonably tight but still kneadable dough. Turn out onto a lightly floured surface and knead for 5–10 minutes until smooth. Form the dough into a rough rectangle, wrap in cling film and place in the fridge for at least 7 hours.

Using a rolling pin, bash the butter on a floured surface to flatten it to a rectangle, 20cm long and just less than 12cm wide. Wrap in cling film and chill in the fridge.

Roll out the chilled dough to a rectangle, 12 x 30cm. Lay the chilled butter on the dough so it covers the bottom two-thirds. Make sure it's positioned neatly and comes almost to the edges of the dough.

Lift the exposed dough at the top and fold down over half of the butter. Fold the butter-covered bottom half of dough over the top. You will now have a sandwich of two layers of butter and three of dough. Seal the edges by pressing or pinching them together. Place in a plastic food bag and chill in the fridge for an hour.

Remove the dough and turn it 90° so you have a short end towards you, then roll it into a long rectangle. Fold the top quarter down and the bottom quarter up so they meet in the middle. Then fold the dough in half along the centre line and press or pinch the edges together to seal. Return to the bag and chill for an hour.

Remove the dough, turn it 90° so a short end is facing you and roll it into a long rectangle. Fold one-third down, then fold the bottom third up over the top. Press or pinch the edges to seal. Return the pastry to the bag and chill for an hour.

Repeat the last stage of rolling, folding and chilling. The dough is now ready to use.

Kneading the dough to develop the gluten.

Bashing the chilled butter with a rolling pin to flatten it to a rectangle, 11.5 x 20cm.

Lifting the butter sheet from the floured surface during flattening to stop it sticking.

Rolling out the chilled dough to a rectangle, 12 x 30cm.

Step photographs continued overleaf

Laying the chilled butter over the bottom two-thirds of the dough.

Folding the top third of the dough down over half of the butter.

Folding the bottom butter-covered third of the dough up over the top.

Bringing the edges together to create a sandwich of three layers of dough and two of butter.

Starting the final roll and fold sequence: rolling out the chilled dough to a long rectangle.

Folding the top third of the dough down over the middle third.

Folding the bottom third of the dough up and over the top.

Giving the dough a quarter-turn (90°) and pressing the edges together to seal.

Hot water crust pastry

MAKES ABOUT 1kg

●●●●●●●●●●●●●

450g plain flour

100g strong white bread flour

75g cold unsalted butter, cut
into roughly 1cm dice

200ml water

½ tsp fine salt

100g lard

Beaten egg yolk, to glaze

I love hot water crust pastry: it's the best thing for a substantial meaty pie, as it keeps the filling moist and tender within its robust, firm crust, which breaks deliciously when you bite into it. The lard gives the pastry a lovely sheen and keeps the pastry impermeable so it can seal in lots of meaty juices without becoming soggy. This quantity is enough for a 20cm raised pie.

Combine the flours in a large bowl. I use a measure of high-gluten bread flour to help give strength to the dough – but not too much or it will become tough.

Add the butter to the flour and rub it in with your fingertips.

Heat the water, salt and lard in a saucepan until just boiling. Immediately pour the liquid onto the flour mixture and briskly mix together with a wooden spoon.

As soon as it's cool enough to handle, gather the warm dough together with one hand, transfer it to a lightly floured surface and quickly knead until smooth.

Your pastry is now ready to use. You need to work fairly quickly with a hot water dough. As the pastry cools, it will become more crumbly and less malleable. Roll it out swiftly (you probably won't need to flour the surface any more as the fat in the dough will stop it sticking) and use it to line your chosen tin, then cover your pie.

I always like to glaze a hot water dough with beaten egg yolk before it goes into the oven, to create a lovely, rich, golden brown sheen.

Rubbing the butter cubes into the flour using the fingertips.

Pouring the boiling water and melted lard mix into the rubbed-in mixture.

Mixing the hot liquid into the flour, using a wooden spoon and working quickly.

Gathering the warm dough to knead until smooth, before quickly rolling out to use.

Suet pastry

MAKES ABOUT 650g
●●●●●●●●●●●●●●●●

285g self-raising flour

1 tsp baking powder

½ tsp fine salt

¼ tsp pepper

125g shredded suet

About 225ml very cold water

Suet pastry is rich and substantial. Although flexible and soft, it's also robust enough to encase a lot of liquid, so it's great for meaty pies or juicy puddings. You'll get a very different finish depending on whether you steam or bake it: either fluffy and tender or crisp and nutty. In days gone by, cooks would have bought chunks of suet (which is the fat from around an animal's kidneys) and chopped or shredded it by hand. These days, you can buy ready-shredded beef suet (or a vegetarian alternative), which is very easy to use. This quantity is enough to line and cover a 1.2 litre pudding basin.

Mix the self-raising flour, baking powder, salt and pepper together in a large bowl. Add the shredded suet and mix thoroughly.

Add most of the water and mix to a soft, slightly sticky dough with one hand, adding more water as necessary. Gather the dough with your hand and transfer it to a lightly floured surface.

Your pastry is now ready to roll out and use; there is no need to chill it first. Suet pastry is best rolled to a 7–8mm thickness.

Adding the shredded suet to the flour and baking powder mixture.

Adding the water to the flour and suet mix.

Gathering the soft, sticky dough with your hands.

Flattening the dough on a lightly floured surface, ready to roll out.

Choux pastry

MAKES A '4-EGG
QUANTITY'
●●●●●●●●●●●●

100g unsalted butter,
cut into roughly 1cm dice
Pinch of salt
300ml water
130g strong white bread flour
4 medium eggs, beaten

This is very different to the other pastries: it's a cooked paste, enriched with lots of egg which is beaten in vigorously to create a glossy dough that puffs up quite dramatically in a hot oven. It's crucial to beat the eggs in a little at a time, so the flour can absorb them, and to beat the dough well to make it smooth, thick and glossy. This quantity is enough to make 6 large buns or 16 éclairs.

Put the butter, salt and water into a large saucepan. Heat gently until the butter has melted, then bring to the boil. (Don't let the liquid boil for any length of time, or you will drive off too much moisture.) Immediately remove from the heat and tip the flour into the pan. Beat with a wooden spoon to form a smooth ball of dough that leaves the sides of the pan clean.

Now vigorously beat the egg into the hot dough, a little at a time. This takes some elbow grease! As you add the egg, the dough will become stiff and glossy. Stop adding the egg if the dough starts to become loose – but you should use up all or most of it.

The dough is now ready to be piped or spooned into puffs, buns or éclairs. Work quickly and get it into a hot oven (190–200°C/gas 5–6) as quickly as possible.

When baked, the pastry should be crisp and dry. As soon as you remove it from the oven, transfer to a cooling rack and split open one side of each piece. This allows steam to escape and stops the pastry becoming soggy. Put the choux on a wire rack to cool.

Beating the flour into the boiling water, salt and butter mixture, off the heat.

Continuing to beat the mixture until it is smooth and leaves the sides of the pan clean.

Vigorously beating the egg into the dough, a small amount at a time.

The finished choux pastry – stiff, glossy and ready to pipe or spoon onto a baking tray.

Rolling out pastry

Rolling out pastry well comes down to confidence: the more often you do it, the better you'll get at it. The trick is to work quickly so the pastry stays cool. Use a good rolling pin (see page 10) and aim for an even thickness throughout. If the pastry crumbles or breaks, don't panic, this probably means it wasn't kneaded quite enough to start with. Just bring it together and re-roll. Don't do this more than once or twice though, or your pastry can become overworked and greasy.

Pastry should be rolled out on a lightly floured surface. If you add too much flour, the pastry will absorb it and become drier and you will also get flour transferred to the filling of your pie or tart. Start with just a light sprinkling on your work surface and your rolling pin, and add a little more as needed.

Use a smooth rolling pin that's not too heavy, as this will let you control the amount of pressure you apply. Roll your pastry with light movements. Roll up from the centre, then down from the centre, give the pastry a quarter turn, dust lightly with more flour and repeat until the pastry has reached the right thickness.

Rolling the pastry down from the centre, using an even, light pressure.

Continuing to roll, having given the pastry a quarter-turn, until it is the required size.

Lining a flan tin

There's something particularly satisfying about lining a tin neatly with pastry. It's a straightforward task, as long as the pastry has been kneaded correctly and rolled out well, and it is not too thick. If the pastry seems fragile and breaks easily, it may be too thin, or too warm. Alternatively, it may need to be re-rolled to bring it together a little more.

To line a flan tin or ring, you'll need the pastry rolled out to roughly a 3mm thickness. If it is much thicker than this, it is unlikely to cook through properly, giving you a soggy, starchy result.

If you are lining a loose-bottomed tin, after you've rolled out your pastry place the base of the tin underneath the pastry. Carefully flip the edges of the pastry into the middle and lift the base into the tin. Now unfold the edges of the pastry, allowing the excess to hang over the sides of the tin.

If you're using a tin (or dish) that doesn't have a loose base, the easiest way to transfer the pastry to the tin is to carefully roll it backwards and loosely onto your rolling pin, then lift it over the tin and carefully unroll it so the pastry falls into the tin.

Use your fingertips to carefully press the pastry down into the tin. You want to avoid stretching the pastry as this will cause it to shrink back in the oven, so gently lift and press it down.

Tear off a small piece of the excess pastry, roughly shape it into a ball and use this to press the pastry into the corners of the tin.

If the pastry case is to be baked blind before filling (see page 42), leave the excess pastry hanging over the sides of the tin (it will be trimmed away later, after baking).

If you are not baking the pastry case blind, trim the edges neatly, with a small, sharp knife.

Folding in the edges of the rolled-out pastry on the metal base before placing in the tin.

Unfolding the pastry, allowing the excess to drape over the sides of the tin.

Pressing the pastry against the sides of the tin, with the fingertips.

Using a small piece of pastry to press the pastry into the corners of the tin.

Baking blind

To ensure the dough cooks through properly, a pastry case is often pre-baked or 'baked blind' before the filling is added. This is particularly important if the filling (such as a custard) needs to be baked at a lower temperature than the pastry requires, which would leave it undercooked in the finished dish.

Blind baking involves covering the uncooked pastry and weighing it down with baking beans. This ensures the pastry bakes snugly into the shape of the tin and doesn't colour too much.

Line your tart tin with pastry, as described on pages 40–1, leaving the excess pastry hanging over the edge. Keep a little uncooked pastry back in case you need to patch any cracks later. It's a good idea to prick the pastry now with a fine-pronged fork, so that any air trapped underneath it can escape without puffing up the pastry.

Line the pastry with a piece of baking parchment or foil (if you scrunch up the parchment first, then smooth it out, it becomes much more malleable).

Fill the pastry case with ceramic baking beans, or uncooked rice or lentils, pressing them gently right to the edge so they hold the pastry in place.

Bake in a hot oven at 200°C/gas 6 for about 15 minutes, then carefully lift out the parchment and baking beans and return the pastry case to the oven for about 8 minutes or until it looks dry and faintly coloured.

Use a small, sharp knife to trim away the excess pastry from the edge. Use a tiny bit of the reserved raw pastry to patch any cracks or holes if necessary.

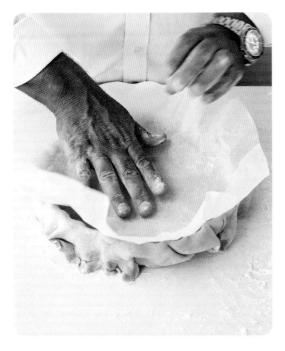

Lining the pastry with a piece of baking parchment.

Filling the parchment-lined pastry case with ceramic baking beans.

The part-baked pastry case with the baking beans and paper removed.

Trimming away the excess pastry from the edge of the pastry case.

SAVOURY

PIES & TARTS

PASTRIES & PORTABLE PIES

THE THING I LOVE about a savoury pie is the way everything is wrapped up in one neat, tasty package. Anything that goes together well on a plate will go well together en croûte. Take my bacon and egg pie, for instance (page 57) – it offers all the flavours of a good cooked breakfast in a single, tasty parcel. Or the lovely lamb and kidney pud on page 87 – you've got meat and gravy, onions and fresh rosemary, all enclosed in a sustaining suet crust.

Pies have been serving us well for hundreds of years, eaten by people from all reaches of society – from kings and queens who ate elaborate raised pies at their banquets, to working men and women who developed pasties to function as portable meals – the pastry protecting and preserving the filling. Pasties were the original fast food, taken down the mines or into factories to provide a filling and balanced meal. That's how recipes like the fabulous Bedfordshire clanger (page 112) evolved, with the main course and pudding encased in the same pastry package.

Even now, the same principles stand. Pies are still incredibly versatile. You can dish them up as an impressive supper or Sunday lunch, but you can also pop a slice or individual pasty in your lunchbox as delicious fuel to get you through a working day.

You should view every pie you make, I think, as a little work of art. That doesn't mean slaving and worrying over it. I promise you that nothing here is difficult or complicated, I just think it's worth taking real pride in your work. Homemade pastry is a world away from the shop-bought, ready-made stuff, and yours will be even better if you relax and enjoy making it. All of the classic pastries used in this chapter are described in detail and illustrated with step-by-step photographs in the Pastry chapter (pages 14–43), so refer back to these if you need to.

It's incredibly satisfying to bring good pastry and a well-made filling together, then slide them into the oven for that final bake where the magic happens, enabling you to bring out something really inviting. Take your time, savour the process and relish the fact that when you make pastry, you're actively continuing a great British culinary tradition.

Corned beef plate pie

SERVES 4–6
●●●●●●●●●

For the shortcrust pastry

300g plain flour

Pinch of salt

75g cold unsalted butter, cut into roughly 1cm dice

75g cold lard, cut into roughly 1cm dice

4–6 tbsp very cold water

1 egg, beaten, to glaze

For the filling

1 tbsp vegetable or sunflower oil

1 medium onion, chopped

1 large carrot, peeled and diced

2 celery sticks, de-stringed and diced

1 large potato, about 250g, such as Desiree, peeled and cut into 1cm dice

340g tin corned beef, broken into large chunks

Splash of Worcestershire sauce

250ml beef stock

1 tbsp chopped parsley

Salt and pepper

Equipment

23cm metal pie plate

This double-crusted pie may have an old-fashioned thrifty feel, but it's ideal for a family supper, and very easy to put together. Use good-quality tinned corned beef for the best flavour and choose a reasonably waxy potato variety such as Desiree that will hold its shape, giving a good texture.

To make the pastry, put the flour into a bowl and mix in the salt. Add the butter and lard and rub into the flour with your fingertips until the mixture resembles fine breadcrumbs. Alternatively, do this in a food processor or mixer and then transfer to a bowl.

Now work in just enough cold water to bring the pastry together. When the dough begins to stick together, use your hands to gently knead it into a ball. Wrap the pastry in cling film and place in the fridge to rest while you make the filling.

Heat the oil in a large frying pan over a medium-low heat. Add the onion, carrot and celery and cook gently for 5–10 minutes until soft but not coloured. Add the potato and cook for another 5 minutes. Next, stir in the corned beef, making sure it's evenly distributed.

Add the Worcestershire sauce, pour over the stock and bring to the boil. Lower the heat and simmer, uncovered, for 20 minutes or so, until the carrot and potato are tender and most of the liquid has evaporated. Taste and add salt and pepper if necessary, then tip into a bowl and leave to cool completely.

Heat your oven to 200°C/gas 6. Have ready a 23cm metal pie plate.

Divide the pastry into two pieces: roughly two-thirds and one-third. Lightly flour your work surface and roll out the larger piece to a 2–3mm thickness. Use to line the pie plate. Roll out the remaining pasty ready to form the lid.

Stir the chopped parsley into the filling. Spoon the filling into the pastry-lined dish (if it's very wet, keep some of the liquid back to serve as gravy). Brush the edges of the pastry on the plate with a little beaten egg then cover the pie with the pastry lid. Crimp the edges together with a fork, or your fingers, then trim away the excess pastry neatly.

Brush the top of the pie with beaten egg and make a hole in the middle to let the steam out. Bake for 30–35 minutes until golden brown. Leave to rest for 15–20 minutes before slicing.

Thai chicken pie

SERVES 6
●●●●●●●

For the shortcrust pastry
150g plain flour
Pinch of fine salt
40g cold unsalted butter, cut into roughly 1cm dice
35g cold lard, cut into roughly 1cm dice
1 tsp lemon juice (optional)
3–4 tbsp very cold water
1 egg, beaten, to glaze

For the filling
2 skinless, boneless chicken thighs, about 150g in total
2 skinless, boneless chicken breasts, about 300g in total
2 tbsp vegetable oil
2 eschalions (banana shallots), chopped
2 garlic cloves, finely chopped
1 red chilli, deseeded and finely chopped
1 tsp finely grated root ginger
2 tsp Thai green curry paste
200ml coconut cream
150ml chicken stock
2 lime leaves
1 lemongrass stem, bruised
1 small sweet potato, about 175g, peeled and cut into 1cm dice
1 tsp cornflour, mixed with a splash of water
A splash of Thai fish sauce
Black pepper

Equipment
1.2 litre pie dish
Pastry lattice cutter

I love a good Thai chicken curry, fragrant with spices, chilli and ginger, and creamy with coconut milk. This is my pastry-topped tribute to that dish.

For the filling, cut all the chicken into 1.5cm chunks. Heat the oil in a sauté pan or wide saucepan over a medium-low heat. Add the shallots, garlic, chilli and ginger and fry gently for a few minutes until soft but not coloured.

Stir in the curry paste and cook for a minute or two. Add the chicken, increase the heat a little and cook, stirring, until it has lost its raw look. Add the coconut cream, chicken stock, lime leaves, lemongrass and sweet potato. Simmer for 12–15 minutes, until the sweet potato is tender.

Add the cornflour liquid, bring to a simmer and stir until the sauce begins to thicken, then take off the heat. Taste the sauce and season with pepper and a little fish sauce. Set aside to cool.

To make the pastry, put the flour and salt in a bowl. Add the diced butter and lard and rub in with your fingertips until the mixture looks like fine breadcrumbs. Alternatively, do this in a food processor or a mixer and then transfer to a bowl.

Now work in just enough cold water to bring the pastry together. When the dough begins to stick together, use your hands to gently knead it into a ball. Wrap the pastry in cling film and place in the fridge to rest for about 30 minutes.

Heat your oven to 200°C/gas 6.

Remove the lemongrass and lime leaves from the cooled pie filling if you prefer and transfer to a 1.2 litre pie dish.

Roll out the pastry on a lightly floured surface and cut a 2cm wide strip of pastry. Dampen the rim of the pie dish with water, press the pastry strip onto it and dampen this too. Use a pastry lattice cutter to cut a pattern in the remaining piece of pastry. Pull the pastry very gently to open up the lattice, then place over the pie. Press the edges down to seal, then trim away the excess pastry.

Brush the top of the pie with beaten egg then bake in the oven for about 30 minutes, until golden. Leave the pie to sit in the tin for 5 minutes before serving, with steamed or stir-fried greens.

Shallot, onion & chive tart

SERVES 4–6
●●●●●●●●●

For the shortcrust pastry

225g plain flour

Pinch of fine salt

60g cold unsalted butter,
cut into roughly 1cm dice

60g cold lard, cut into roughly
1cm dice

3–5 tbsp very cold water

For the filling

8 eschalions (banana shallots)

3 large onions, halved

25g unsalted butter

1 tbsp sunflower oil

4 medium eggs

2 medium egg yolks

200ml double cream

1½ tbsp wholegrain mustard

1 tbsp chopped chives

Salt and pepper

Equipment

23cm loose-based fluted tart
tin, 3.5cm deep

Three different alliums give this creamy tart a lovely range of savoury flavours, while the grainy mustard adds a note of sweetness. Like most savoury egg tarts, it is best eaten warm or at room temperature, rather than piping hot.

To make the pastry, put the flour into a bowl and mix in the salt. Add the butter and lard and rub into the flour with your fingertips until the mixture resembles fine breadcrumbs. Alternatively, do this in a food processor or mixer and then transfer to a bowl.

Now work in just enough cold water to bring the dough together. When it begins to stick together, gently knead it into a ball. Wrap in cling film and chill in the fridge for around 30 minutes.

Meanwhile, for the filling, thinly slice the shallots and onions. Heat the butter and oil in a large frying pan over a medium-low heat. Add the shallots and onions with a pinch of salt and cook slowly for at least 20 minutes, stirring occasionally, until they are very soft and golden. Season with pepper and more salt if needed. Leave to cool.

Heat your oven to 200°C/gas 6 and have ready a 23cm loose-based fluted tart tin, 3.5cm deep.

Roll out the pastry on a lightly floured surface to a 3mm thickness and use it to line the tart tin, leaving the excess hanging over the edge. Keep a little uncooked pastry back in case you need to patch any cracks later. Prick the pastry base with a fork. Line the pastry with baking parchment or foil and then fill with baking beans, or uncooked rice or lentils.

Bake blind for 15 minutes, then remove the parchment and baking beans and return the pastry to the oven for about 8 minutes or until it looks dry and faintly coloured. Trim away the excess pastry from the edge. Use a tiny bit of the reserved raw pastry to patch any cracks or holes if necessary. Turn the oven down to 180°C/gas 4.

For the filling, whisk the eggs, egg yolks and cream together, then whisk in the mustard and chives. Season with salt and white pepper.

Spoon the cooled onion mixture into the pastry case and spread it evenly, then carefully pour on the egg mixture. Bake in the oven for 30–35 minutes, until the filling is just set and golden. Leave in the tin for 5 minutes, then unmould. Serve warm or cold.

Step photographs overleaf

Slicing the shallots and onions for the filling.

Setting aside the golden, softened slow-cooked shallots and onions to cool.

Whisking the eggs, egg yolks and cream together for the filling.

Spooning the cooled shallots and onions into the blind-baked pastry case.

Pouring the whisked egg, chive and mustard mixture into the pastry case.

Bacon & egg pie

SERVES 6
●●●●●●●

For the rich shortcrust pastry
275g plain flour
Pinch of fine salt
135g cold unsalted butter, diced
1 medium egg, beaten
1 tsp lemon juice
2–3 tbsp very cold water
1 egg, beaten, to glaze

For the filling
1 tbsp vegetable oil
1 large onion, finely chopped
1 garlic clove, crushed
200g unsmoked streaky
bacon, diced
200g pork loin, cut into
roughly 1.5cm dice
5 medium eggs
100g cream cheese
100g mature Cheddar, grated
1 tbsp chopped chives
Salt and pepper

Equipment
20cm loose-based sandwich
tin, 4cm deep

This is a delicious savoury pie that really makes the most of a winning partnership. I love the way the whole eggs are hidden beneath the crust – if you get one when you cut into it, it's like gaining a prize. Serve this hot for supper or cold for lunch.

To make the pastry, put the flour and salt in a bowl. Add the diced butter and rub in with your fingertips until the mixture looks like fine breadcrumbs. Alternatively, do this in a food processor or a mixer and then transfer to a bowl.

Mix the egg with the lemon juice and 2 tbsp water. Make a well in the centre of the rubbed-in mixture and pour in the egg mix. Mix the liquid into the flour and fat mixture, using one hand; avoid overworking the dough. If it is too dry, add a splash more water. When the dough begins to stick together, use your hands to gently knead it into a ball. Wrap the pastry in cling film and place in the fridge to rest for about 30 minutes.

For the filling, heat the oil in a wide frying pan over a medium-low heat and add the onion and garlic. Cook gently for about 8 minutes, until soft. Add the bacon and pork, increase the heat a little, and cook for about 10 minutes, stirring from time to time, until any liquid from the meat has been driven off. Leave to cool completely.

Heat your oven to 200°C/gas 6 and have ready a 20cm loose-based sandwich cake tin, 4cm deep.

Beat two of the eggs with the cream cheese until smooth. Add the Cheddar and chives and season with salt and pepper. Stir in the cooled bacon mixture.

Roll out two-thirds of the pastry and use to line the cake tin. Roll out the remaining pastry ready to form the lid.

Put the filling mixture into the pastry case. Make 3 evenly spaced depressions in the filling and crack the remaining eggs into them.

Brush the rim of the pastry with water and place the lid on top. Press the edges to seal and trim off the excess neatly. Brush the top of the pie with beaten egg and make a steam hole in the centre.

Bake in the oven for 50–55 minutes, until golden brown. Leave the pie to settle for at least 15 minutes before cutting. It is delicious hot or cold.

Pork, apple & cider pie

SERVES 4

●●●●●●●

For the cider pastry

1 medium egg, beaten

125ml dry cider

125ml olive oil

1 tsp baking powder

Pinch of fine salt

350–400g plain flour

1 egg, beaten, to glaze

For the filling

1–2 tbsp vegetable oil

1 medium-large onion, chopped

2 celery sticks, de-stringed and chopped

500g pork shoulder, cut into 3–4cm pieces

2 tbsp plain flour

175ml dry cider

175ml chicken stock

1 cooking apple, about 150g, peeled, cored and sliced

2 eating apples, 225–250g in total, peeled, cored and sliced

6 large sage leaves, chopped

Salt and pepper

Equipment

1.2 litre pie dish

Pie funnel

This gorgeous pie plays on the wonderful affinity between pork and apples. The fruit gives a subtle sweetness to the cider-enriched gravy and sage lends an aromatic note.

First make the filling. Heat 1 tbsp oil in a large, wide pan over a medium-low heat. Add the onion and celery and cook gently for 8–10 minutes, until soft but not coloured. Remove the vegetables from the pan.

Add a little more oil if necessary, increase the heat to medium-high and add half the pork. Brown it well on all sides, remove from the pan and repeat with the remaining pork.

Turn the heat down a little. Return all the pork to the pan with the onion and celery. Sprinkle in the flour, stir and cook for 1 minute. Gradually add the cider and stock, stirring them in so the flour is absorbed. Add the apples and sage. Bring to the boil, reduce the heat and simmer for about 45 minutes, until the pork is tender. Taste the sauce and season with salt and pepper. Leave to cool.

To make the pastry, beat the egg in a large bowl with the cider, olive oil, baking powder and salt. Slowly mix in the flour until you have a soft dough. You may not need all the flour. Wrap the dough in cling film and leave to rest in the fridge for 30 minutes.

Heat your oven to 200°C/gas 6.

Position a pie funnel in the middle of a 1.2 litre pie dish and spoon the filling into the dish.

On a lightly floured surface, roll out the pastry to a 3mm thickness. Cut a 2cm wide strip from the pastry. Dampen the rim of the pie dish with water. Press the pastry strip onto the rim and dampen this too. Lift the pastry sheet over the pie and press down the edges to seal. Trim off the excess pastry and make a steam hole in the centre of the pie, exposing the funnel. Crimp the edges. Cut leaves and shape little berries from the pastry trimmings to decorate the pie.

Brush the pastry lid with beaten egg. Arrange the pastry leaves and berries on top of the pie and brush these with egg too. Bake for 35–40 minutes until the pastry is crisp and golden.

Let stand for 10–15 minutes before serving, with mash and greens.

Step photographs overleaf

Pork, apple & cider pie

Spooning the pork and apple filling into the pie
dish around the pie funnel.

Pressing the strip of pastry onto the dampened rim of the pie dish.

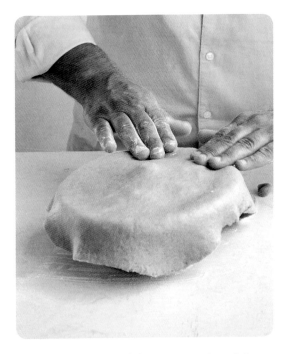

Pressing the edges of the positioned pie lid onto the pastry strip to seal the pie.

Trimming off the excess pastry from the edge of the pie.

Crimping the edges of the pastry by pinching between your thumbs and forefingers.

Smoked haddock & watercress tart

SERVES 4–6
●●●●●●●●●

For the black pepper pastry

200g plain flour

Pinch of fine salt

½ tsp coarsely ground black pepper

50g cold unsalted butter, cut into roughly 1cm dice

50g cold lard, cut into roughly 1cm dice

1 tsp lemon juice (optional)

3–5 tbsp very cold water

For the filling

250g smoked haddock fillet

200ml whole milk

1 bay leaf

25g unsalted butter

25g plain flour

2 medium eggs, beaten

Small bunch of spring onions, finely sliced

30g watercress, stalks removed

25g fine white breadcrumbs

25g finely grated Parmesan

Finely grated zest of 1 lemon

Equipment

36 x 12cm loose-based fluted tart tin, 3cm deep, or a 23cm round tart tin

Savoury tarts need a punchy, well-flavoured filling. Smoked fish and peppery watercress fit the bill nicely and a crunchy, golden crumb topping is a lovely contrast to the creamy sauce beneath.

To make the pastry, mix the flour with the salt and pepper in a large bowl. Add the butter and lard and rub in with your fingertips until the mixture resembles fine breadcrumbs. Alternatively, do this in a food processor or mixer and then transfer to a bowl.

Mix the lemon juice, if using, with 3 tbsp water. Using one hand, work the liquid into the flour, adding a little more water if needed, just until the pastry clumps together. Gently knead into a ball, wrap in cling film and rest in the fridge for about 30 minutes.

Heat your oven to 200°C/gas 6 and have ready a 36 x 12cm loose-based fluted tart tin, 3cm deep, or a 23cm round tart tin.

Roll out the pastry on a lightly floured surface to a 3mm thickness and use to line the tart tin, leaving the excess overhanging the edge. Keep a little uncooked pastry back to patch any cracks later. Prick the pastry base with a fork. Line the pastry with baking parchment or foil then fill with baking beans, or uncooked rice or lentils.

Bake blind for 15 minutes, then remove the paper and beans and return the pastry to the oven for about 8 minutes or until it looks dry and faintly coloured. Trim away the excess pastry from the edge and patch any cracks or holes with raw pastry if necessary.

Meanwhile, for the filling, put the fish in a saucepan, pour on the milk and add the bay leaf. Bring to a simmer, turn the fish over and simmer gently for about 2 minutes, until it is just cooked. Lift out the fish and set aside. Discard the bay leaf. Pour the milk into a jug.

In the same pan, melt the butter over a low heat and stir in the flour. Cook, stirring, for 2 minutes, then take off the heat. Gradually beat in the warm milk until you have a smooth, thick sauce. Return to the heat and cook gently for 2–3 minutes, stirring often. Let cool for a few minutes. Stir in the beaten eggs, then the spring onions.

Flake the fish into bite-sized chunks, discarding any skin and bones. Scatter the fish in the pastry case, top with the watercress and pour over the sauce. Mix the breadcrumbs with the Parmesan and lemon zest and scatter over the filling. Bake for 20 minutes until the crust is golden brown. Let cool slightly in the tin, then serve with a salad.

Cheese, potato & onion pie

SERVES 6

●●●●●●●

For the cheese pastry

200g plain flour

75g cold unsalted butter,
cut into roughly 1cm dice

75g white vegetable fat,
cut into small pieces

25g Parmesan, finely grated

25g mature Cheddar,
finely grated

2–3 tbsp very cold water

1 egg, beaten, to glaze

For the filling

1kg Desiree potatoes

1 medium onion, finely diced

375g mature Cheddar, grated

50ml milk

2 tbsp chopped chives

Salt and white pepper

Equipment

24 x 20cm metal baking dish,
5cm deep

I used to buy pies like this in my local chip shop, as a lad. Based on potatoes with lots of full-flavoured cheese, it's warming and filling – real comfort food. The rich pastry is very tender and almost melts into the filling beneath. Serve as a meat-free main course, with some steamed greens or a big bowl of salad.

To make the pastry, put the flour into a bowl. Add the butter and vegetable fat and rub them in with your fingertips until the mixture looks like coarse breadcrumbs (this dough is richer and stickier than a standard pastry). Alternatively, rub in the fat using a food processor or a mixer and then transfer to a bowl.

Add the cheeses to the flour and fat and mix well. Now, using one hand, work in just enough cold water to bring the pastry together into a dough. When the dough begins to stick together, gently knead it into a ball. Wrap in cling film and place in the fridge to chill while you make the filling.

Heat your oven to 200°C/gas 6 and have ready a metal baking dish, about 24 x 20cm and 5cm deep.

For the filling, peel the potatoes and cut them into large chunks. Place in a saucepan, cover with water, add a little salt and bring to the boil. Reduce to a simmer and cook until the potatoes are tender enough to mash – probably 12–15 minutes. Drain the potatoes well and put them through a ricer into a large bowl (this will give you smooth, lump-free mash but you can use a standard potato masher).

Add the onion, cheese, some salt and a good pinch of white pepper. Beat with a wooden spoon so the cheese is well incorporated. Add the milk and chives and give the mix a good stir.

Put the cheesy mash mixture into the tin and spread it out with the back of a spoon until smooth and even.

On a lightly floured surface, roll out the pastry so it will just fit on top of the mash. It should be 8–10mm thick. Place it on top of the mash, trim the edges neatly and mark the pastry into 6 portions by scoring with a knife.

Brush the pastry with beaten egg and bake for 20–25 minutes until the crust is golden. Let the pie stand for 15 minutes before cutting and serving.

Rabbit & pancetta pot pies

●●●●●●●

For the flaky pastry

175g plain flour

Pinch of fine salt

65g cold unsalted butter,
cut into 5mm–1cm dice

65g cold lard, cut into
5mm–1cm dice

1 tsp lemon juice

130ml very cold water

1 egg, beaten, to glaze

For the filling

1 tbsp sunflower oil

25g unsalted butter

2 rabbits (1.5–2kg total), jointed

175g diced pancetta

1 onion, sliced

1 garlic clove, sliced

1 fennel bulb, trimmed
and sliced

175ml white wine

600ml chicken stock

1 bay leaf

300ml double cream

2 tbsp chopped parsley

Salt and black pepper

Equipment

4 individual pie dishes

I kept rabbits as a child and was so distraught when a fox got them that I didn't eat rabbit until my thirties! I've since found it makes a great pie filling, with a little pancetta to balance its leanness. Make this warming, hearty dish during autumn and winter when you'll really appreciate it and rabbit is at its best.

Make the pastry following the recipe on page 24. Wrap the dough in cling film and chill in the fridge while you make the filling.

Heat a large sauté pan over a high heat and add the oil and butter. Working in batches, brown the rabbit well all over (include the liver and kidneys, if you have them, for extra flavour). Remove from the pan and set aside. Add the pancetta to the pan, reduce the heat a little and cook for 4 minutes or until golden and beginning to crisp around the edges. Add to the rabbit.

Turn the heat to low. Add the onion, garlic and fennel to the pan and cook gently for 2–3 minutes. Add the wine, increase the heat and let it bubble for a couple of minutes, scraping the base of the pan with a spatula to release any caramelised bits. Return the rabbit and pancetta to the pan. Add the stock and bay leaf, bring to a simmer, cover and simmer gently for 1½ hours, until the rabbit is tender.

Remove the rabbit from the pan and leave until cool enough to handle, then strip the meat from the bones and put into a large bowl.

Bring the contents of the pan to the boil, and boil to reduce the liquid by half. Stir in the cream and bring back to the boil. Add the parsley, taste the sauce and season with salt and pepper as required. Return the rabbit meat to the pan and turn to coat in the sauce. Divide the filling between 4 individual pie dishes. Leave to cool.

Heat your oven to 200°C/gas 6.

On a lightly floured surface, roll out the pastry to a 5mm thickness and cut lids for the pies, using the dishes as guides. Brush the rim of each dish with beaten egg and position the pie lids. Press the edges to seal and trim off the excess. Crimp the edges. Make a slit in the top of each pie lid and brush the pastry with beaten egg.

Bake for 20–30 minutes until the pastry is golden brown and the filling bubbling. Leave to settle for 10 minutes or so, then serve, with plain boiled potatoes, carrots and a green vegetable.

Step photographs overleaf

Rabbit & pancetta pot pies

Browning the rabbit joints for the filling.

Adding the wine to the softened onion, garlic and fennel and letting it bubble away.

Stripping the rabbit from the bones.

Adding the cream to the sauce for the filling.

Cutting the lids for the pies, using the dishes as a guide and allowing excess all round.

Positioning the pie lids over the filling.

Crimping the edges decoratively with the thumb and forefinger.

Cutting a slit in the top of the pie to allow steam to escape.

Buffalo & ale pie

SERVES 4–6

●●●●●●●●●

For the flaky pastry

175g plain flour

Pinch of fine salt

65g cold unsalted butter, cut into 5mm–1cm dice

65g cold lard, cut into 5mm–1cm dice

1 tsp lemon juice

130ml very cold water

1 egg, beaten, to glaze

For the filling

2 tbsp plain flour

1kg buffalo stewing steak, cut into 4–5cm cubes

1–2 tbsp vegetable oil

25g unsalted butter

12 shallots, peeled but left whole

2 large carrots, peeled and cut into 2cm slices

2 tsp mushroom ketchup

1 tbsp tomato purée

300ml ale or stout

300ml beef stock

Few thyme sprigs

1 tsp soft dark brown sugar

Salt and pepper

Equipment

1.5 litre pie dish

Pie funnel

Water buffalo are now farmed in this country. Their meat makes a delicious alternative to beef: it's lean and cooks to a lovely tenderness, with a rich flavour. If you can't get hold of buffalo, you can use good stewing beef such as braising or chuck steak (simmer it for about twice as long before putting in the pie).

Make the flaky pastry following the recipe on page 24. Wrap in cling film and chill in the fridge while you make the filling.

Put the flour in a large bowl and season it well with salt and pepper. Toss the meat in the flour until evenly coated.

Heat 1 tbsp oil and the butter in a flameproof casserole over a medium-high heat. Working in batches, brown the meat well all over, adding a dash more oil if you need to. Transfer the browned meat to a dish.

Lower the heat under the pan, add a little more oil if necessary and add the shallots and carrots. Sauté for a couple of minutes, until the shallots are just starting to soften. Return all the meat to the pan. Add the mushroom ketchup and tomato purée and cook for another 2 minutes.

Pour in the ale and stock, then add the thyme and sugar. Bring to the boil, then reduce the heat, cover with a lid and simmer gently for 1 hour or until the meat is very tender. Leave to cool completely.

Position a pie funnel in the middle of a 1.5 litre pie dish and spoon the filling into the dish. (If there is a lot of liquid, keep some of it back to serve as gravy.)

Heat your oven to 200°C/gas 6.

On a lightly floured surface, roll out the pastry to a 3mm thickness. Cut a 2cm wide strip of pastry. Dampen the rim of the pie dish with water and press the pastry strip onto the rim; dampen this too. Cut the remaining pastry a little larger than the pie dish. Position the lid over the filling, press the edges to seal and crimp them. Trim away the excess pastry.

Brush the pastry with beaten egg and make a steam hole in the middle, exposing the funnel. Bake for 35-40 minutes until the pastry is crisp and golden. Leave to settle for 10-15 minutes before serving.

Sausage plait

SERVES 6
● ● ● ● ● ● ●

For the puff pastry

100g strong white bread flour

100g plain flour

Pinch of fine salt

75–100ml cold water

165g cold unsalted butter

1 egg, beaten, to glaze

For the filling

300g chestnut mushrooms, trimmed

2 tbsp thyme leaves

1 tbsp sunflower oil

25g unsalted butter

2 red onions, thinly sliced

2 tsp soft brown sugar

1 tbsp sherry vinegar

300g good-quality sausagemeat (or skinned butcher's sausages)

100g black pudding, cut into 1–2cm pieces

1 tbsp sesame seeds

Salt and pepper

Equipment

Large baking sheet (lipped)

This is either a poor man's Wellington, or a posh sausage roll, depending on how you look at it. It's certainly good enough for a special meal. The sausage filling is spiked with black pudding, enhanced with a savoury mushroom base and topped with caramelised onions. Wrapped in crisp, buttery 'plaited' pastry, it looks really impressive yet it's easy to make.

Make the puff pastry following the recipe on page 28. Wrap in cling film and chill in the fridge while you prepare the filling.

Put the mushrooms in a food processor, season with salt and pepper and pulse until reduced to a rough paste. Add the thyme and give the mix a final pulse. Transfer to a dry frying pan and cook over a medium-high heat, stirring often, until all the liquid has evaporated from the mushrooms. Remove from the pan and set aside to cool.

Heat the oil and butter in a wide frying pan on a medium-low heat. Add the onions with the sugar and cook slowly until soft and lightly caramelised. This will take at least 20 minutes. Stir in the sherry vinegar and set aside to cool.

Heat your oven to 200°C/gas 6. Line a large lipped baking sheet with baking parchment (some butter may leak out of the pastry).

Roll out the pastry to a rectangle, about 26 x 30cm. Spread the mushroom paste down the middle third of the pastry, leaving a 5cm gap at the top and bottom.

Mix the sausagemeat with the black pudding, mould into a long sausage shape that will fit on top of the mushroom paste and place it on the paste. Spread the caramelised onions on top of it.

Cut slits on the diagonal all the way down the pastry on each side of the filling at 2cm intervals. Brush lightly with egg. Take one strip over the filling from one side, then one from the other and so on, crossing the strips over to form a plaited effect. Tuck the ends of the pastry under the plait, trimming off excess if necessary. Using a large palette knife, carefully lift onto the prepared baking sheet.

Brush the plait with beaten egg and sprinkle with sesame seeds. Bake for 30 minutes or until the pastry is golden brown. Leave to settle for 10 minutes or so, then serve hot or cold. This is delicious with a dollop of apple sauce on the side.

Step photographs overleaf

Sausage plait

Spreading the mushroom paste down the middle of the pastry.

Positioning the sausagemeat and black pudding mixture on the mushroom paste.

Cutting slits in the sides of the pastry, on the diagonal, at 2cm intervals.

Brushing the pastry on either side of the filling lightly with beaten egg.

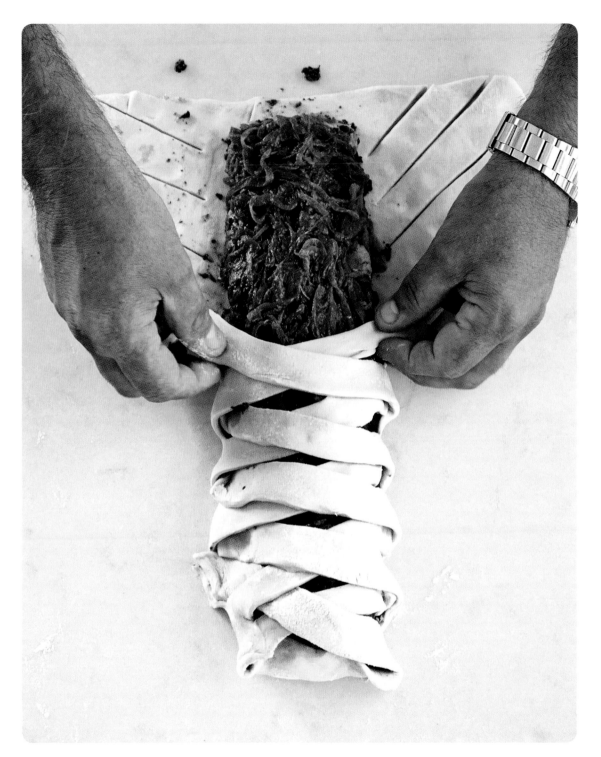

Crossing the strips of pastry over the filling to
give a plaited effect.

Hollywood's temptation

SERVES 4–6
●●●●●●●●●

75g unsalted butter

1 large onion, thinly sliced

800g waxy potatoes, such
as Maris Peer, peeled and
thinly sliced

About 500ml whole milk

4 large sheets of filo pastry
(about 25 x 40cm each)

400g hot-smoked salmon
fillet, flaked

100ml double cream

Salt and pepper

Equipment

20cm springform cake tin,
7cm deep

Baking sheet (lipped)

This recipe is based on a Swedish gratin-style dish called Janssen's Temptation, which pairs potatoes with sprats or anchovies. I like to use hot-smoked Scottish salmon instead, combining it with thinly sliced potatoes, sweet onion and cream, then encasing the whole lot in crisp filo pastry to give a contrasting texture.

Heat 25g of the butter in a large frying pan. Add the onion and sweat gently over a low heat for around 20 minutes, stirring often, until very soft and golden. Season with a little salt and pepper and set aside.

Put the sliced potatoes in a large saucepan and pour on enough milk to cover. Bring to the boil, lower the heat and simmer for about 5 minutes until the potatoes are just tender but not cooked through. Drain the potatoes, reserving 100ml of the milk.

Heat your oven to 200°C/gas 6 and put in a lipped baking sheet (as the pie may leak a little butter) to heat up. Use a little of the butter to grease a 20cm springform cake tin, about 7cm deep.

Melt the remaining butter. Brush a sheet of filo pastry with melted butter and place, butter-side up, in the cake tin, leaving the excess hanging over the side. Turn the cake tin slightly, then lay another sheet of filo in the tin at an angle to the first sheet and brush it with melted butter. Repeat to use the rest of the filo sheets, brushing with butter as you layer them in the tin.

Put one-third of the potatoes into the pastry-lined tin and season with a little salt and pepper. Follow with half the onions and then half the flaked fish. Repeat these layers, then finish off with the final third of potato.

Mix the reserved milk with the cream and pour over the filling.

Fold the overhanging pastry back over the filling to enclose it, and brush the top of the pie with melted butter. Place the pie on the hot baking sheet in the oven and bake for 30–35 minutes until the filo is crisp and golden.

Leave the pie to stand for 30 minutes or so – it's best eaten warm or at room temperature – then transfer to a large plate before slicing.

Step photographs overleaf

Hollywood's temptation

Brushing the first sheet of filo with melted butter and laying in the prepared cake tin.

Layering the sheets of filo in the tin, to line it fully and evenly.

Brushing the layers of filo with melted butter as they are layered in the tin.

Scattering half the golden, softened onions over the potato layer in the bottom of the filo case.

Layering half of the flaked salmon over the onion layer.

Adding the second layer of sliced potatoes.

Folding the overhanging filo over the top of the filling to seal the pie.

Brushing the top of the pie with melted butter before baking.

Raised game pie

SERVES 8
●●●●●●●●

For the hot water crust pastry
100g lard, plus extra for
greasing
450g plain flour
100g strong white bread flour
75g cold unsalted butter,
cut into roughly 1cm dice
200ml water
½ tsp salt
1 egg yolk, beaten, to glaze

For the filling
2 eschalions (banana shallots),
finely chopped
2 garlic cloves, crushed
700g mixed, boned, diced
game meat, such as venison,
rabbit, pheasant, pigeon
and/or boar
200g minced pork belly
200g back bacon, rind
removed, diced
2 tbsp Madeira
½ tsp ground mace
½ tsp ground allspice
2 tbsp chopped parsley
2 tbsp chopped thyme
Salt and white pepper

Equipment
20cm springform cake tin,
about 7cm deep

A game pie makes a spectacular centrepiece and this handsome example is amazingly straightforward – especially if you buy mixed game meat ready-prepared from a good butcher. Don't be daunted by the idea of using hot water crust pastry either – the pie is moulded in a tin, which makes it very easy to put together.

Heat your oven to 200°C/gas 6. Grease a 20cm springform cake tin, about 7cm deep, with lard.

First make the filling. Put the shallots and garlic into a large bowl. Add the game, pork belly mince, diced bacon, Madeira, spices and herbs. Season with salt and a little white pepper. Using your hands, mix all the ingredients thoroughly together. Put in the fridge while you prepare the pastry.

To make the pastry, combine the flours in a bowl, add the butter and rub in with your fingertips. Heat the water, salt and lard in a pan until just boiling. Pour the mixture onto the flour and mix together with a wooden spoon. Once cool enough to handle, tip onto a lightly floured surface and knead to a smooth dough.

Work as quickly as you can now (as the pastry will become more crumbly as it cools). Cut off two-thirds of the pastry, roll it out and use to line the prepared tin, leaving any excess hanging over the side. Check there are no cracks or holes in the pastry. Roll out the remaining pastry for the lid and leave to one side.

Spoon the filling into the pastry-lined tin. Press it down and level the surface.

Brush the edge of the pastry in the tin with beaten egg yolk and place the pastry lid on top. Press the edges together to seal and trim off the excess pastry neatly. Crimp the edges decoratively. Make a couple of slits in the top of the pie to allow steam to escape and brush the pastry with egg yolk.

Stand the tin on a baking tray and bake the pie for 30 minutes. Then turn the oven down to 160°C/gas 3 and bake for a further 1¾ hours.

Leave the pie to cool completely in the tin before removing. Slice on a plate to catch any juices. Serve at room temperature.

Step photographs overleaf

Raised game pie

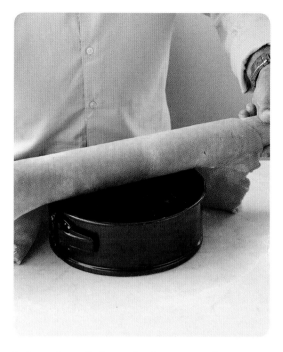

Lifting the rolled two-thirds portion of pastry into the cake tin to line the base and sides.

Pressing the pastry into the sides of the tin, making sure there are no cracks or holes.

Spooning the filling into the pastry-lined tin.

Positioning the pie lid over the filling.

Pressing the edges of the pastry together to seal the pie.

Trimming away the excess pastry from the edge of the tin.

Crimping the edges decoratively using the thumb and forefinger.

Cutting slits in the top of the pie to allow steam to escape.

Raised pork & egg pie

SERVES 8
●●●●●●●●

For the hot water crust pastry

100g lard, plus extra for greasing

450g plain flour

100g strong white bread flour

75g cold unsalted butter, cut into roughly 1cm dice

200ml water

½ tsp salt

1 egg yolk, beaten, to glaze

For the filling

300g good-quality sausagemeat (or skinned butcher's sausages)

300g minced pork

150g cooked ham hock, cut into roughly 1.5cm pieces

2 eschalions (banana shallots), finely chopped

3 tbsp chopped parsley

4 hard-boiled eggs, shelled

Salt and white pepper

Equipment

1kg loaf tin (about 10 x 20cm base measurement)

I love pies that have the treat of whole eggs hidden inside. This is a picnic classic and a slice would be great in a lunchbox too.

Heat your oven to 200°C/gas 6. Grease a 1kg loaf tin (measuring about 10 x 20cm across the base) with lard, then strip-line it with baking parchment (i.e. cut one long strip of parchment, the width of the tin, and place it in the tin so that there's an overhang of parchment at each end, which will help you remove the pie later).

First make the filling. Put all the ingredients, except the hard-boiled eggs, into a large bowl, seasoning lightly. Mix together thoroughly (the easiest way to do this is with your hands). Cook a little nugget of the mixture in a frying pan and taste it to check the seasoning. Put the mix in the fridge while you make the pastry.

To make the pastry, combine the flours in a bowl, add the butter and rub in lightly with your fingertips. Heat the water, salt and lard in a saucepan until just boiling. Pour the mixture onto the flour and mix together with a wooden spoon. Once cool enough to handle, tip onto a lightly floured surface and knead to a smooth dough.

Working quickly (the pastry will become crumbly and more difficult to handle as it cools), roll out two-thirds of the pastry and use it to line the prepared tin, leaving the excess hanging over the edges.

Press half the meat filling into the pastry-lined tin. Take a thin slice off the top and bottom of each boiled egg (this helps them sit next to each other and makes slicing the pie easier), then place the eggs lengthways down the middle of the pie. Add the remaining meat filling and pat it down.

Brush the overhanging pastry edge with egg yolk. Roll out the remaining pastry to make a lid, place over the pie and trim away the excess. Pinch the pastry edges together to seal and crimp neatly. Cut leaves from the pastry trimmings to decorate the pie.

Brush the pastry lid with beaten egg and make a couple of steam holes in the centre. Arrange the pastry decorations on top of the pie and brush these with egg too.

Bake for 30 minutes then reduce the heat to 180°C/gas 4 and bake for a further hour. Leave to cool completely in the tin. To remove the pie, turn the tin on its side and use the parchment paper to slide out the pie. Serve in thick slices.

Lamb & kidney suet pudding with rosemary

SERVES 4–6

●●●●●●●●●

For the suet pastry

Butter for greasing

285g self-raising flour

125g shredded suet

1 tsp baking powder

1 tbsp finely chopped rosemary

About 225ml very cold water

For the filling

30g unsalted butter

2–3 tbsp vegetable oil

2 eschalions (banana shallots), sliced

2 garlic cloves, sliced

1 tbsp plain flour

1 tbsp finely chopped rosemary

500g lamb shoulder, trimmed and diced into bite-sized pieces

3 lamb's kidneys, halved, tough white core removed, cut into bite-sized pieces

150ml red wine

150ml rich beef stock

Salt and pepper

Equipment

1.2 litre pudding basin

When it comes to comfort food, you just can't beat a traditional steamed suet pudding like this one. It takes a little while to cook but is very simple to put together. Here I am using flavour-rich shoulder of lamb for the filling, with aromatic rosemary, shallots and garlic. If you would prefer a classic steak and kidney pud, see the variation (overleaf).

First make the filling. Melt the butter with 1 tbsp oil in a large, wide heavy-based saucepan over a medium-low heat. When it is foaming, add the shallots and garlic and cook for a few minutes until they begin to soften, but not colour.

Meanwhile, in a large bowl, mix the 1 tbsp flour with the chopped rosemary and some salt and pepper. Add the lamb and kidneys and toss them thoroughly in the seasoned flour.

Transfer the softened shallots and garlic to a large bowl and set to one side. Add a little more oil to the pan and increase the heat. Add a third of the lamb and kidneys and cook until browned all over. Set aside with the shallots and repeat with the remaining meat, adding more oil if needed. Return all the meat and the shallots to the pan.

Add the wine to the pan and let it bubble and reduce for a couple of minutes, scraping the base of the pan with a spatula to help release any caramelised bits. Add the stock and simmer for 5 minutes. If the sauce looks too thick, add a little water. Taste the sauce and season with salt and pepper. Set aside to cool completely.

When you are ready to cook the pudding, first generously butter a 1.2 litre pudding basin.

To make the suet pastry, mix the flour, suet, baking powder and rosemary together in a bowl and season with salt and pepper. Add most of the water and mix to a soft, slightly sticky dough with one hand, adding more water as necessary. Divide the dough into two pieces – roughly three-quarters and one-quarter.

Dust your work surface with flour and roll out the larger piece of dough into a circle, roughly 30cm in diameter. Use this to line the pudding basin, leaving the excess pastry hanging over the edge.

Continued overleaf

Lamb & kidney suet pudding

Lifting the rolled three-quarters portion of suet pastry into the greased pudding basin to line it.

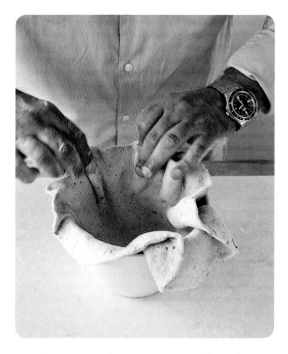

Gently pressing the pastry against the sides of the basin, allowing the excess to overhang.

The pastry-lined pudding basin, ready to fill.

Spooning in the cooled filling.

Step photographs continued overleaf

Roll out the small piece of dough to a circle, large enough to form a lid for the basin. Spoon the cooled filling into the pastry-lined basin. Dampen the edge of the pastry in the bowl with water and position the pastry lid. Press the edges together and trim away the excess pastry neatly. Crimp the edges to ensure a good seal.

Place a large piece of baking parchment on a sheet of foil on your work surface and make a large pleat in the middle, folding both sheets together (this allows for the pudding's expansion as it cooks). Lay the parchment and foil over the top of the pudding basin, foil side up, and secure with string, looping the end of the string over the top of the pudding and tying it to form a handle that will enable you to lift the pudding in and out of the saucepan.

Stand the pudding basin in a large pan, and pour in enough boiling water to come halfway up the side of the basin. Put a tight-fitting lid on the pan and bring to a simmer. Lower the heat to maintain a simmer and steam the pudding for 2–2½ hours. Top up the boiling water during steaming if necessary so the pan doesn't boil dry.

Lift the pudding basin out of the pan, remove the foil and parchment and leave to rest for 5 minutes. Then run the tip of a small, sharp knife around the side of the pudding to release it from the basin. Invert a large, deep plate over the pudding and turn the plate and pudding over, so the pudding comes out onto the plate.

Serve straight away, with mashed potato and a green vegetable such as broccoli or leafy greens.

Variation: Steak & kidney pudding

Instead of the lamb, use 500g chuck (or braising) steak and 3 calf's kidneys, cut into bite-sized pieces. Dust the steak and kidneys with seasoned flour. Melt 30g butter with 1 tbsp oil in a heavy-based pan and gently cook 1 sliced large onion until beginning to soften but not colour. Remove from the pan and set aside. Add a little more oil to the pan and increase the heat. Brown the beef and kidneys all over in batches. Once it is all browned, return all the meat and the onion to the pan and pour in 150ml red wine. Let it bubble to reduce a little, then add 150ml rich beef stock. Taste the sauce and season as required. Leave the filling to go cold. Make the suet pastry and continue as above.

Positioning the pastry lid.

Pressing the edges of the pastry lid onto the dampened rim of the lining pastry to seal.

Trimming away the excess pastry.

The crimped, sealed pudding, ready for steaming.

Covering a pudding for steaming

Laying the pleated foil and parchment on top of the pudding.

Securing the foil and parchment in position with string.

Tying the string under the rim, leaving a length to loop over the basin and tie to create a handle.

The covered pudding ready for steaming.

Meat & potato pie

SERVES 4
●●●●●●●

For the suet crust
375g self-raising flour
175g shredded beef suet
About 250ml very cold water

For the filling
2 large onions, chopped
700g chuck steak (braising steak), cut into 4–5cm chunks
400g waxy potatoes, such as Estima or Maris Peer, peeled and cut into 4cm chunks
400g floury potatoes, such as King Edward, peeled and cut into 4cm chunks
Salt and pepper

Equipment
1.2 litre pie dish

This no-nonsense recipe is one of my favourite pies. I use chuck steak (often sold as braising steak) which has lots of flavour, and two types of potato: a floury variety, which falls apart and thickens the gravy, and a waxier type that holds its shape to provide texture.

First make the filling. Put the onions and steak in a large pan. Add enough water to just cover them and bring to a simmer. Cover with a lid, reduce the heat and simmer very gently for 1½ hours.

Add the potatoes to the pan, along with some salt and pepper, and cook for a further 30–35 minutes or until the potatoes are soft and the meat is tender. The gravy should be nicely thickened by the potatoes. Check the seasoning.

Pour off 300–600ml of liquid from the pan – enough to leave the filling nicely moist but not swimming in liquid – and save this to serve as gravy with the pie. Transfer the filling to a 1.2 litre pie dish and leave to cool completely.

Heat your oven to 200°C/gas 6.

To make the suet pastry, combine the flour and suet in a large bowl with some salt and pepper. Add most of the water and mix to a soft, slightly sticky dough with one hand, adding more water as needed. Leave to stand for 5 minutes.

On a lightly floured surface, roll out the dough to around a 7–8mm thickness. Cut a 2cm wide strip of pastry. Dampen the rim of the pie dish with water. Stick the pastry strip onto the rim and dampen this too. Lay the sheet of pastry on top. Press down the edges to seal and crimp or flute them, trimming off the excess pastry.

Bake the pie for 30–40 minutes until the pastry is golden brown. Leave to stand for 10–15 minutes before serving.

Chilli beef cornbread pies

SERVES 4–6
●●●●●●●●●

For the filling

About 2 tbsp sunflower oil

500g shin of beef, trimmed
and cut into 1cm cubes

1 large onion, diced

2 garlic cloves, crushed

1 red chilli, finely chopped

1 tsp dried oregano

½ tsp cocoa powder

1 tbsp tomato purée

400g tin chopped tomatoes

200ml rich beef stock

400g tin kidney beans, drained
and rinsed

3 large roasted red peppers
from a jar, roughly chopped

Good pinch of chilli powder
(optional)

Salt and black pepper

For the cornbread topping

125g plain flour

125g cornmeal

½ tsp salt

115g unsalted butter, melted
and slightly cooled

2 medium eggs, beaten

250ml buttermilk

1 green chilli, deseeded and
very finely chopped

½ tsp baking powder

120g strong Cheddar, grated

Equipment

4–6 individual pie dishes

Freshly baked cornbread is a great accompaniment to stews and chilli and this recipe combines the two elements in one golden, bubbling dish. Shin of beef is a very economical cut – it needs a good, long cook to make it tender, but you'll be rewarded with a fantastic depth of flavour.

To make the filling (which you can do ahead of time), first heat your oven to 170°C/gas 3.

Heat about 1 tbsp oil in a flameproof casserole over a medium-high heat. Add half the beef and brown it well. Remove and set aside in a dish. Add the remaining meat, and a little more oil if necessary, brown it and remove from the pan.

Reduce the heat to medium-low and add a little more oil to the pan. Add the onion and garlic and cook for 5–8 minutes, until softened.

Add the chilli, oregano, cocoa powder and tomato purée to the onions and stir to mix. Return the meat to the pan, along with any juices that have seeped from it, and cook for a few minutes. Season with salt and pepper.

Add the tomatoes and beef stock, bring to a simmer, then cover and cook in the oven for 1 hour. Add the kidney beans and peppers and return to the oven for a further hour or until the meat is tender.

Check the seasoning (if it's not hot enough for you, you can spice it up with a little chilli powder) then spoon the mixture into 4–6 deep, individual pie dishes, leaving about 2cm below the rim.

Turn the oven up to 180°C/gas 4.

To make the cornbread batter, mix the flour, cornmeal and salt in a large bowl. Combine the melted butter, eggs, buttermilk, green chilli and baking powder in a jug. Add to the dry ingredients and mix just until combined. Don't overmix.

Top the chilli beef with the cornbread batter, then sprinkle cheese over each dish. Bake for about 30 minutes, until golden. If you like, you can finish the pies under the grill for a few minutes to get a really nice golden brown top. Serve straight away.

Luxury fish pie

SERVES 6

For the poaching stock

600ml fish stock

600ml water

50ml Pernod

1 small onion, roughly chopped

1 small fennel bulb, roughly chopped

2 celery sticks, roughly chopped

1 bay leaf

Few parsley sprigs

For the filling

500g haddock fillet (or other white fish of your choice), skinned

250g salmon fillet, skinned

250g smoked langoustine tails

For the saffron mash

1.5kg floury potatoes, such as King Edward, peeled and cut into large chunks

100ml double cream

Good pinch of saffron strands

50g unsalted butter

For the sauce

40g unsalted butter

40g plain flour

300ml reserved poaching stock

100ml double cream

2 tbsp chopped tarragon

Salt and pepper

Equipment

1.5-2 litre ovenproof dish

A good fish pie, I think, always needs some smoked fish – or shellfish – to give it a real depth of flavour and what could be more luxurious than smoked Scottish langoustines? If you can't get hold of any, use giant tiger prawns instead, and replace half the plain haddock with smoked haddock.

Heat your oven to 200°C/gas 6. Have ready a large ovenproof dish, 1.5-2 litres capacity.

Place all the ingredients for the poaching stock in a large pan and bring to the boil. Reduce the heat to a simmer and add the haddock and salmon. Poach the fish for a few minutes, until it is just cooked. Strain the mixture, reserving all the liquid. Pick out and discard the stock vegetables. Leave the fish to cool.

Put the poaching liquid into a clean pan. Bring to the boil, and boil until the liquid has reduced by half. You will need 400ml of this reduced liquor. Set aside.

For the saffron mash, put the potatoes in a large saucepan, cover with cold water, add a little salt and bring to the boil. Lower the heat and simmer for 15-20 minutes, until tender.

Meanwhile, to make the sauce, melt the butter in a pan. Stir in the flour to form a roux. Let this cook over a medium heat, stirring often, for 2-3 minutes. Turn the heat down very low and gradually add the reduced poaching liquid, a ladleful at a time, beating well after each addition to create a smooth sauce. Return to the heat and cook, stirring often, for about 5 minutes. Stir in the cream, tarragon and some salt and pepper.

Drain the potatoes well. Heat the cream, saffron and butter gently in the potato pan, until the butter has melted, then take off the heat and pass the potatoes through a ricer into the pan (or just tip them in and mash). Season well with salt and pepper and stir to combine.

Flake the cooked fish evenly over the base of your ovenproof dish, checking for any bones as you go. Scatter over the langoustines. Pour over the sauce. Top with the mash, spread it evenly and then mark decoratively with a fork.

Bake for 25-30 minutes until golden brown on top and bubbling all the way through. If your assembled pie has cooled down, it may take longer. Serve with buttered peas.

Goat-herd pie

SERVES 4

●●●●●●●

For the filling

1–2 tbsp olive oil

2 medium onions, finely diced

2 celery sticks, de-stringed and diced

125g butternut squash, peeled and diced

2 garlic cloves, peeled

½ tsp coarse sea salt

4 anchovy fillets in oil, drained

500g goat mince

1 tbsp tomato purée

1 tbsp plain flour

1 tbsp roughly chopped green olives

150ml red wine

150ml beef stock

1 tbsp chopped rosemary

½ tsp ground cinnamon

Salt and pepper

For the topping

1kg floury potatoes, such as King Edward, peeled and cut into chunks

50g unsalted butter

25g crumbly goat's cheese, crumbled

25g Parmesan, finely grated

To finish (optional)

Extra grated Parmesan

Equipment

1.2 litre ovenproof dish

We've all heard of shepherd's pie. It's a dish thought to have originated in the sheep-farming country of northern England and, though the title itself is not recorded until Queen Victoria's time, the dish probably dates back much further. Some early versions were doubtless very basic but it's a recipe that's been embellished and perfected by generations of cooks. This recipe uses goat meat instead of lamb, which is a leaner meat and very tasty indeed. You can, of course, still use lamb if you prefer.

To make the filling, heat 1 tbsp olive oil in a wide frying pan over a medium-low heat. Add the onions, celery and squash and cook gently for about 10 minutes, until the onions begin to soften.

Using a pestle and mortar, crush the garlic with the salt to a paste. Add the anchovies and bash to form a rough paste, then add this mixture to the pan of vegetables. Cook gently for about 5 minutes, stirring, so the anchovies begin to 'melt' into the vegetables. Spoon the contents of the pan into a bowl, leaving any oil behind.

Increase the heat under the pan. Add a little more oil if necessary, and half the mince. Cook, stirring, until it is browned, then add it to the vegetables. Repeat with the remaining mince, then return all the meat and vegetables to the pan.

Stir in the tomato purée and flour and cook gently for 2–3 minutes. Add the olives and pour in the wine and stock. Bring to the boil, then lower the heat and simmer for 15 minutes. Add the rosemary and cinnamon and season with pepper, and a little salt if needed (the anchovies are already quite salty).

Transfer the filling to an ovenproof dish, about 1.2 litre capacity.

Heat your oven to 190°C/gas 5.

For the topping, put the potatoes in a saucepan, cover with water, add a little salt and bring to the boil. Lower the heat and simmer for 15–20 minutes, until the potatoes are tender. Drain well, mash or rice them back into the hot pan and stir in the butter.

Spread the mash over the meat in the dish. Combine the crumbled goat's cheese and Parmesan and sprinkle over the potato. Bake for 25–30 minutes until the top is golden and crusty and the filling is bubbling. Leave to stand for 10–15 minutes before serving, sprinkled with a little extra Parmesan if you like. Serve with a green vegetable.

Spinach, feta & pine nut parcels

MAKES 4
●●●●●●●

For the dough
250g strong white bread flour
1 tsp fine salt
1 tsp fast-action dried yeast
2 tbsp olive oil, plus extra for
kneading
125–150ml water

For the filling
1 tbsp olive oil
2 garlic cloves, crushed
500g frozen whole-leaf
(not chopped) spinach
125g Yorkshire Fettle cheese,
or feta, crumbled
2 tbsp pine nuts, lightly toasted
3 tbsp chopped mint
Salt and black pepper

Equipment
Baking tray
18cm plate

These triangular pasties are based on a Lebanese speciality called *fatayer* and use soft bread dough, rather than pastry, to enclose the filling. I prefer frozen spinach for this recipe – it's very easy to use and actually produces a less watery mixture.

To make the dough, put the flour into a large bowl and add the salt to one side and the yeast to the other. Add the olive oil and pour in 125ml of the water. Start to mix with the fingers of one hand, adding a little more water as you go, gradually incorporating all the flour from the side of the bowl until you have a rough dough. It should be soft and slightly sticky. You may not need to add all the water or you may need a bit more (depending on the absorbency of the flour).

Trickle a little olive oil onto your work surface and knead the dough on it for a good 5 minutes until it becomes smooth and is no longer sticky. Return to the bowl and cover with cling film. Leave it in a warm place for about an hour until doubled in size and puffy.

Meanwhile, make the filling. Heat the olive oil in a wide frying pan over a low heat, add the garlic and cook gently for a minute or until just starting to colour. Transfer to a large bowl. Now add the frozen spinach to the pan and turn the heat up high. Cook, stirring often, until the spinach is soft and all the liquid released has evaporated. Add to the bowl with the garlic and season with pepper and a pinch of salt (remember that the cheese will be very salty). Leave to cool, then add the cheese, pine nuts and mint. Mix thoroughly.

When you are ready to assemble the parcels, heat your oven to 220°C/gas 7 and line a baking tray with baking parchment.

Transfer the risen dough to a lightly floured surface and deflate it gently, then roll it out to a 5mm thickness. Using a plate as a guide, cut out 4 circles, 18cm in diameter.

Divide the filling between the circles, forming it into a pyramid shape in the centre. Dampen the pastry margin with water. Bring the dough up over each side of the triangle of filling, forming a pyramid shape. Pinch the edges of the dough together with your fingers to seal. Trim off any excess and press together again.

Put the spinach parcels on the prepared baking tray and bake for 12–15 minutes until golden. Eat hot, warm or cold.

Step photographs overleaf

Spinach, feta & pine nut parcels

The risen dough, ready for rolling out.

Rolling and smoothing out the deflated dough to a 5mm thickness.

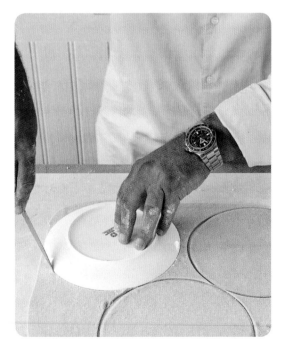

Using a plate as a template to cut out 18cm dough circles.

Removing the pastry trimmings.

Dividing the filling between the circles and forming it into a pyramid shape.

Bringing the dough up over two sides of the triangle of filling to join over the top.

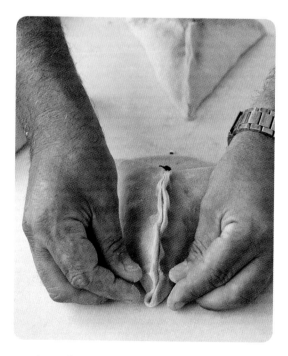

Pinching the edges together between thumbs and forefingers to seal.

The triangular parcel ready to bake, with the third side of dough sealed over the filling.

Chicken & chorizo empanadas

MAKES 10

● ● ● ● ● ● ●

For the empanada dough
150g unsalted butter
300g plain flour
Large pinch of fine salt
1 medium egg, lightly beaten
3–5 tbsp water

For the filling
4 chicken thighs, on the bone
and skin on
1 tbsp olive oil
1 medium onion, finely
chopped
1 garlic clove, crushed
100g cured chorizo sausage
(ready-to-eat), finely diced
½ tsp cumin seeds
50g raisins
Salt and pepper

To finish
1 egg, beaten, to glaze

Equipment
Large baking sheet
12cm cutter or bowl

Traditional in Spain, Portugal and Latin America, empanadas are little pastry pockets with an intensely flavoured savoury filling. They are great eaten any time but make a particularly good tapas-style snack with a cold beer.

Heat your oven to 180°C/gas 4. For the filling, put the chicken thighs in a small roasting dish, season well all over with salt and pepper and roast for about 45 minutes until cooked through. Set aside to cool a little.

Meanwhile, make the pastry. Melt the butter and leave it to cool slightly. Put the flour into a large bowl and mix in the salt. Pour in the butter and egg. Start mixing, adding the water as you go, until you have a soft dough. Turn out onto your work surface and knead gently for a couple of minutes, until smooth. Return the dough to its bowl, cover and set aside to rest while you prepare the filling.

Heat the olive oil in a frying pan over a medium-low heat. Add the onion and cook for 10–12 minutes, until soft. Add the garlic, chorizo, cumin seeds and raisins. Cook over a medium heat for 5–8 minutes, stirring often, until the chorizo is cooked. Remove from the heat.

Once the chicken thighs are cool enough to handle, remove the skin. Pull all the meat from the bones and chop it roughly. Add to the chorizo mixture. Taste and add salt and pepper if needed (the chorizo is already quite salty), then leave to cool completely.

Turn the oven up to 200°C/gas 6 and line a large baking sheet with baking parchment.

Lightly flour your work surface and roll out the dough to a 3–4mm thickness. Using a 12cm cutter, or a small bowl as a guide, cut out 10 discs. You will probably need to re-roll the offcuts once to get this many. Divide the filling between the discs. Dampen the edges of the dough with water, then fold over one half of each disc to make a semi-circular parcel. Press the edges together firmly, then crimp or press the edges with a fork.

Put the empanadas on the baking sheet and brush with beaten egg. Bake for 15–20 minutes, until golden. Eat them warm, on their own or with a chilli sauce.

Savoury choux buns with creamy mushrooms

SERVES 6

●●●●●●●

For the choux buns

100g unsalted butter, cut into
roughly 1cm cubes

Pinch of fine salt

300ml water

130g strong white bread flour

1 tbsp chopped thyme

4 medium eggs, beaten

25g Parmesan, finely grated

For the filling

25g unsalted butter

1 tbsp olive oil

1 large eschalion
(banana shallot), sliced

600g mixed mushrooms,
roughly chopped

2 garlic cloves, chopped

1 tsp thyme leaves

2 tbsp dry sherry

200g crème fraîche

Juice of ½ lemon

1 tbsp chopped flat-leaf parsley

Salt and pepper

Equipment

Baking tray

This recipe has a retro feel about it, and it's none the worse for that. The deliciously savoury flavours here, and the beautifully crisp choux pastry, will always go down a storm.

Heat your oven to 220°C/gas 7 and line a baking tray with baking parchment.

To make the choux buns, put the butter, salt and water into a large saucepan. Heat gently until the butter has melted then bring to the boil. Immediately remove from the heat and tip in the flour and thyme. Beat with a wooden spoon to form a smooth ball of dough that should leave the sides of the pan.

Now vigorously beat the beaten eggs into the hot dough, a little at a time. This takes some elbow grease! As you do so, the dough will become stiff and glossy. Stop adding the egg if the dough starts to become loose – but you should use up all or most of it.

Spoon the dough into 6 large blobs, each about 7cm in diameter, on the prepared baking tray. (Alternatively, you can pipe the choux onto the tray.) Sprinkle the Parmesan evenly on top of them.

Bake in the centre of the oven for 10 minutes until the choux buns are well risen and golden. Then turn the oven down to 190°C/gas 5 and bake for a further 30 minutes to ensure the centres are cooked. The buns should be crisp and dry. On removing from the oven, split one side of each bun open to allow the steam to escape. Transfer to a wire rack to cool.

For the filling, melt the butter with the oil in a large, wide frying pan. Add the shallot and cook for a few minutes until soft but not coloured. Add the mushrooms, garlic and thyme. Cook over a high heat for about 10 minutes, stirring often, until the mushrooms are buttery, soft and reduced in volume by about half, and their liquid has been driven off.

Add the sherry and crème fraîche and allow to bubble gently for about 10 minutes to reduce the sauce. Stir in the lemon juice and parsley and season with salt and plenty of black pepper.

Cut each choux bun fully in half. Fill with the warm mushroom mixture and serve, with a green salad.

Scotch pies

MAKES 8
●●●●●●●

For the hot water crust pastry
720g plain flour

320ml water

1 tsp fine salt

240g lard

1 egg yolk, beaten, to glaze

For the filling
1.2kg minced mutton

½ tsp ground mace

½ tsp freshly grated nutmeg

150ml gravy or stock

Salt and white pepper

Equipment
Large baking tray

18cm plate

10cm saucer

Also known as mutton pies, these have a long history. In the Middle Ages, they were viewed as luxurious, decadent English-style food and frowned upon by the Scottish church. As time moved on, they proved to be convenient, sustaining snacks for working people, who would buy them hot from pie-men or pie-wives in the city streets. The space in the top of the pie, created by the raised crust, would sometimes be filled with gravy, beans or mashed potato.

Line a large baking tray with baking parchment.

First make the filling. Mix the ingredients together, seasoning well and working the liquid into the meat. Divide into 8 portions and mould each into a ball. Refrigerate while you make the pastry.

Have ready 8 strips of baking parchment, about 5cm deep and 25cm long, to wrap around the pies, and 8 lengths of string to secure them.

For the pastry, put the flour into a bowl. Heat the water, salt and lard in a saucepan until just boiling. Pour the mixture onto the flour and mix together with a wooden spoon. Once cool enough to handle, tip onto a lightly floured surface and knead to a smooth dough.

Working quickly, cut off a quarter of the pastry and set aside. Roll out the remaining dough to a 5mm thickness and cut out 8 circles, 18cm in diameter, using a plate as a guide. Roll out the remaining pastry and cut out 8 lids, 10cm in diameter, using a saucer as a guide.

Place a ball of filling on each large pastry circle. Gather the pastry around the meat and bring up the sides to form the shape of a pork pie, stretching the pastry so it comes above the meat by about 2cm.

Dampen the edges of the pies with water and press the lids on top of the filling. Seal the edges together with your fingers. Wrap a strip of parchment around the pie and secure with string, to make sure the pie holds its shape when cooked. You will find this easier to do if you have someone to help you. Repeat until you have 8 pies.

Put the pies on the baking tray and cut a steam hole in the centre of each. Brush with egg yolk. Leave to rest in the fridge for 30 minutes.

Meanwhile, heat your oven to 200°C/gas 6. Bake the pies for 35–40 minutes until golden brown. Serve hot.

Step photographs overleaf

Scotch pies

Quickly rolling out the pastry, while it is still warm and pliable.

Cutting out 18cm circles, using a plate as a guide.

Placing a ball of filling in the centre of each pastry circle.

Bringing the pastry up around the filling.

Positioning the pie lids.

Tying a band of parchment around each pie to ensure it holds its shape on baking.

Cutting a steam vent in the middle of each pie.

Brushing the tops of the pies with beaten egg yolk to glaze.

Bedfordshire clangers

MAKES 4
●●●●●●●

For the suet pastry

300g self-raising flour

1 tsp fine salt

100g beef suet

50g cold unsalted butter,
cut into roughly 1cm dice

About 200ml very cold water

1 egg, beaten, to glaze

For the savoury filling

1 tbsp vegetable oil

25g unsalted butter

1 small leek, trimmed,
quartered lengthways and
thinly sliced

1 large potato, about 250g,
peeled and cut into 5mm dice

175g uncooked gammon, cut
into 1cm cubes

1 tsp English mustard

Salt and pepper

For the sweet filling

50g soft brown sugar

1 small cooking apple, about
150g, peeled, cored and diced

1 pear, about 150g, peeled,
cored and diced

50g sultanas

½ tsp ground cinnamon

15g unsalted butter, cut into
4 pieces

Equipment

Large baking sheet (lipped)

These pies have a savoury filling at one end and a sweet one at the other. They used to function as complete, portable meals for farm labourers – the savoury portion would be marked by three steam holes and the sweet with two, so everyone knew which end to eat first. The name may come from an old Midlands word 'clanging', which means 'eating with great relish'.

First make the savoury filling. Heat the oil and butter in a frying pan over a medium heat. Add the leek and potato and cook gently for about 5 minutes, until the leek is soft. Add the gammon and cook for another 5 minutes, until it is just cooked. Take off the heat and stir in the mustard and some salt and pepper. Leave to cool.

To make the sweet filling, just mix all the ingredients, except the butter, together in a bowl.

Heat your oven to 220°C/gas 7. Line a large lipped baking sheet with baking parchment.

For the pastry, mix the flour, salt and suet in a bowl. Add the butter and rub in lightly with your fingertips until the mix resembles breadcrumbs. Stir in just enough cold water to form a soft dough.

To assemble, lightly dust a work surface with flour and roll out the dough to about 60 x 25cm. Now cut across into 4 rectangles, about 25 x 15cm. Trim the edges so they are neat and straight, then roll the trimmings from each portion of dough into a little sausage.

Brush a line of beaten egg across the middle of each piece of pastry and lay the pastry sausage on it. Pinch to form a 'dam' which will keep the fillings separate. Put one quarter of the savoury filling on one half of each piece of pastry and one quarter of the sweet on the other. Top the sweet filling with a dot of butter.

Brush the pastry edges with beaten egg. Fold the pastry over the fillings to form a long sausage roll shape. Press either side of the central pastry 'dam' and press the edges together to seal. Make three diagonal slashes on the savoury ends and two on the sweet. Transfer to the baking sheet, seam side down, and brush with egg.

Bake for 15 minutes, then turn the oven down to 180°C/gas 4 and bake for a further 20 minutes. Serve the clangers hot or cold.

Step photographs overleaf

Bedfordshire clangers

Cutting the pastry into 4 rectangles, each about 25 x 15cm.

Trimming the pastry edges to ensure they are straight and neat.

Positioning a pastry 'sausage' along the middle of each pastry rectangle.

Pinching the pastry sausage to form a ridge that will keep the savoury and sweet fillings separate.

Brushing the edges of the pastry around the fillings with beaten egg.

Folding the pastry over the fillings to enclose them and form a long sausage roll shape.

Pressing either side of the central pastry divider towards the middle to ensure a good seal.

Cutting three slashes on the savoury ends and two on the sweet ends (to identify them).

SWEET

PIES & TARTS

HOT PUDDINGS

COLD PUDDINGS

CAKES & PASTRIES

PUDDINGS MAY BE INDULGENT but that doesn't mean we shouldn't enjoy them. I'm a firm believer that a little of what you fancy does you good. I would rather skip the starter than miss out on pudding. In fact, I am one of those pud lovers who looks at the dessert menu first in a restaurant, so I can decide how much room I need to leave!

I've seen traditional puddings like the ones in this book make a real comeback in recent years, not that they ever really went away – they have been on the menu of every 5-star hotel I've ever worked in. But more and more home cooks are looking for recipes like these, the kind of timeless comfort puds that take us all back to our childhoods. It makes sense: if you can turn out a beautiful steamed sponge or a classic treacle tart, you're on to a winner. They are what I call class-breakers: everyone likes them, no matter their background.

Baked puddings have always been a big part of my life. My Nan was a great pudding cook and I have fond memories of her fruit pies and tapioca puds. She even used to make little chocolate puds similar to my chocolate volcanoes (page 176), though she cooked them for a little bit longer so the filling was not so molten. The nostalgic appeal of these dishes partly explains their popularity, but there's more to them than that. They are, or at least they can be, truly delicious. They've become classics for a reason.

These recipes are straightforward: good, simple baking. To start with, you may find it helpful to refer back to my step-by-step guides to the individual pastries in the Pastry chapter (pages 14–43) when you are making one of the tarts or pies. In time, they will become second nature.

The secret to success is to use the very best ingredients you can. I think cooks can sometimes be a bit blasé about 'basic' items like flour, sugar and butter, but these are the absolute mainstay of most puddings and the quality is crucial. Start out with good ingredients, weigh and measure with care, and you can expect great results.

Apple & Wensleydale pie

SERVES 6

●●●●●●

For the shortcrust pastry

350g plain flour

175g cold unsalted butter,
cut into roughly 1cm dice,
plus extra for greasing

About 75ml very cold water

For the filling

500g cooking apples

500g eating apples

100g caster sugar

125g Wensleydale cheese,
crumbled

To finish

A little milk

About 1 tbsp granulated sugar

Equipment

26 x 20cm baking tin, about
4cm deep

There's a saying in Yorkshire that 'apple pie without cheese is like a kiss without a squeeze'. I couldn't agree more – tangy, salty cheese and sweet apple go beautifully together. I like to use a mixture of cooking and eating apples in this pie, in order to create a varied, interesting texture.

To make the pastry, put the flour in a bowl. Add the diced butter and rub it in with your fingertips until the mixture looks like fine breadcrumbs. Alternatively, do this in a food processor or a mixer and then transfer to a bowl.

Now work in just enough cold water to bring the pastry together, using one hand. When the dough begins to stick together, gently knead it into a ball. Wrap the pastry in cling film and rest in the fridge for about 30 minutes.

Heat your oven to 200°C/gas 6. Lightly butter a baking tin, about 26 x 20cm and about 4cm deep.

For the filling, peel, quarter and core all of the apples. Slice them into a large bowl and toss together.

Once the dough has rested, cut it into two pieces, roughly one-third and two-thirds. Lightly dust your work surface with flour. Roll out the larger piece of pastry so it's a good 6cm larger all round than the base of the tin. Line the base and sides of the tin with the pastry, leaving the excess hanging over the sides.

Lay a third of the apple slices in the pastry-lined tin and sprinkle with a third of the sugar. Repeat with the remaining apple and sugar. Now scatter the crumbled cheese evenly over the fruit.

Roll out the remaining pastry to make a lid. Brush the edges of the pastry in the tin with milk, then put the pastry lid on top. Seal the edges with your fingertips and crimp them; trim off the excess pastry neatly. Brush the pastry with milk and sprinkle with sugar. Make two slits in the top to allow steam to escape.

Bake for 30–35 minutes or until the crust is golden brown. Leave to stand for at least 15 minutes before slicing. The pie is delicious hot or cold and needs no accompaniment.

French-style apple tart

SERVES 6

For the sweet shortcrust

200g plain flour

2 tbsp icing sugar

100g cold unsalted butter,
cut into roughly 1cm dice

1 medium egg, lightly beaten

1 tsp lemon juice

2 tbsp very cold water

For the frangipane

100g unsalted butter, softened

100g caster sugar

2 medium eggs

50g plain flour

75g ground almonds

2–3 drops of almond extract

For the apples

3 medium eating apples

15g cold butter, cut into small
pieces

1½ tbsp caster sugar

4 tbsp sieved apricot jam,
to finish

Equipment

25cm loose-based fluted tart
tin, 3cm deep

Inspired by the wonderful *tarte aux pommes* of Normandy, this is a beautiful way to show off the flavours of our home-grown apples too. The apples – tender and caramelised but holding their shape – are cushioned on a soft, almondy frangipane layer and finished with an apricot glaze.

To make the pastry, mix the flour and icing sugar together in a bowl. Add the diced butter and rub it in with your fingertips until the mixture looks like fine breadcrumbs. Alternatively, do this in a food processor or a mixer and then transfer to a bowl.

Mix the egg with the lemon juice and water. Make a well in the centre of the flour mixture and pour in the egg mix. Using one hand, work the liquid into the flour to bring the pastry together. If it seems too dry, add a splash more water. When the dough begins to stick together, gently knead it into a ball. Wrap in cling film and rest in the fridge for at least 15 minutes.

Heat your oven to 200°C/gas 6 and put a baking tray in to heat up. Have ready a 25cm loose-based fluted tart tin, 3cm deep.

Roll out the pastry on a lightly floured surface to about a 3mm thickness and use it to line the tart tin. Trim the edge neatly and prick the base of the pastry with a fork.

To make the frangipane, cream the butter and sugar together until soft and fluffy. Beat in the eggs, one at a time, then mix in the flour, ground almonds and almond extract. Spread the frangipane over the pastry base, smoothing it out evenly.

Peel, core and thinly slice the apples. Starting at the edge and working towards the centre, lay them, overlapping, on top of the frangipane. Dot with the 15g cold butter. Place on the hot tray in the oven and bake for 15 minutes. The tart will be starting to brown.

Sprinkle the sugar over the apples, then return to the oven for 10–15 minutes, until the sugar has melted and caramelised.

While still warm, heat the apricot jam very gently with a splash of water, to make a glaze, and brush it over the apples. Leave the tart to cool completely, then serve with crème fraîche, or whipped or clotted cream.

Step photographs overleaf

French-style apple tart

Combining the ingredients for the frangipane.

Spreading the frangipane evenly over the base of the pastry case with the back of a spoon.

Thinly slicing the apples for the filling.

Arranging the apple slices in a circular pattern over the frangipane.

Glazing the warm tart with sieved apricot jam
after baking.

Cobnut, pear & sticky toffee tart

SERVES 8
●●●●●●●●

For the sweet shortcrust

200g plain flour

2 tbsp icing sugar

100g cold unsalted butter,
cut into roughly 1cm dice

1 medium egg, lightly beaten

1 tsp lemon juice

2 tbsp very cold water

For the filling

200g stoned dates, roughly
chopped

150ml whole milk

3 ripe medium pears, about
500g in total

50g unsalted butter, softened

1 tsp vanilla extract

100g plain flour

1 tsp bicarbonate of soda

50g ground almonds

2 large eggs

100g light muscovado sugar

2 tbsp treacle

100g shelled cobnuts or
hazelnuts, roughly chopped

For the toffee sauce

200g light muscovado sugar

50g unsalted butter

250ml double cream

Equipment

25cm loose-based fluted tart
tin, 3.5cm deep

Kentish cobs are cultivated hazelnuts, often larger than the wild variety, and easier to gather. Crunchy and sweet, they partner apples and pears perfectly in this autumnal, nutty, treacly tart.

To make the pastry, mix the flour and icing sugar together in a bowl. Add the diced butter and rub it in with your fingertips until the mixture looks like fine breadcrumbs. Alternatively, do this in a food processor or a mixer and then transfer to a bowl.

Mix the egg with the lemon juice and water. Make a well in the centre of the flour mixture and pour in the egg mix. Using one hand, work the liquid into the flour to bring the pastry together. If it seems too dry, add a splash more water. When the dough begins to stick together, gently knead it into a ball. Wrap in cling film and rest in the fridge for at least 15 minutes.

For the filling, put the chopped dates and milk in a pan. Bring to the boil, and then set aside for 30 minutes to soak.

To make the toffee sauce, heat the sugar, butter and cream together in a pan over a low heat until melted and smooth, then bring to a simmer and let bubble for 5 minutes to thicken. Leave to cool.

Heat your oven to 180°C/gas 4 and put in a baking tray to warm up. Have ready a 25cm loose-based fluted tart tin, 3.5cm deep.

Roll out the pastry on a lightly floured surface and use it to line the tart tin. Prick the base with a fork. Peel, quarter and core the pears; slice each quarter in two. Arrange in a circular pattern in the tart case. Drizzle over 4 tbsp of the toffee sauce and place in the fridge while you prepare the rest of the filling.

Mash the date mixture to a coarse purée with a potato masher. Tip it into a bowl with the softened butter, vanilla, flour, bicarbonate of soda, ground almonds, eggs, sugar and treacle. Whisk together with an electric whisk until just combined. Stir in the chopped nuts.

Spoon the date and nut mixture over the pears in the pastry case, spreading it out evenly. Bake the tart on the hot baking tray for 40–45 minutes, until the filling is well risen and browned. Leave to stand for 10 minutes before removing from the tin.

Serve the tart warm, with clotted cream or ice cream and the rest of the toffee sauce.

Yorkshire curd tart

SERVES 6

●●●●●●●●

For the sweet shortcrust

150g plain flour

2 tbsp icing sugar

75g cold unsalted butter,
cut into roughly 1cm dice

1 egg yolk

½ tsp lemon juice

1 tbsp very cold water

For the filling

50g caster sugar

225g curd cheese

2 medium eggs

2 medium egg yolks

Finely grated zest of 1 lemon

1 tsp rosewater

25g unsalted butter, melted

50g currants

½ tsp freshly grated nutmeg

Equipment

20cm loose-based sandwich
cake tin, 2–3cm deep

Curd tarts were traditionally baked for Whitsuntide, when many Yorkshire villages held feasts and fair days. The filling was originally made from 'beestings', the first, very rich milk from newly calved cows, though nowadays it's easier (and just as good) to use curd cheese. Rosewater is a classic flavouring.

For the pastry, mix the flour and icing sugar together in a bowl. Add the diced butter and rub it in with your fingertips until the mixture looks like fine breadcrumbs. Alternatively, do this in a food processor or a mixer and then transfer to a bowl.

Mix the egg yolk with the lemon juice and water. Make a well in the centre of the flour mixture and pour in the egg mix. Using one hand, work the liquid into the flour to bring the pastry together. If it seems too dry, add a splash more water. When the dough begins to stick together, gently knead it into a ball. Wrap in cling film and rest in the fridge for at least 15 minutes.

Heat your oven to 200°C/gas 6 and have ready a 20cm loose-based sandwich cake tin, 2–3cm deep.

Roll out the pastry on a lightly floured surface to about a 3mm thickness and use it to line the tart tin, leaving the excess pastry hanging over the edge. Keep a little uncooked pastry back in case you need to patch any cracks later. Prick the base with a fork.

Line the pastry case with baking parchment or foil, then fill with baking beans, or uncooked rice or lentils. Bake blind for 15 minutes, then remove the parchment and baking beans and return to the oven for about 8 minutes or until the pastry looks dry and faintly coloured. Use a small, sharp knife to trim away the excess pastry from the edge. Use a tiny bit of the reserved raw pastry to patch any cracks or holes if necessary. Turn the oven down to 180°C/gas 4.

To make the filling, beat the sugar and curd cheese together until smooth, then beat in the eggs and egg yolks, lemon zest, rosewater and melted butter. Stir in the currants.

Pour the filling into the pastry case and grate a little nutmeg over the surface. Bake for about 20 minutes, until the filling is just set. Leave to cool completely in the tin before slicing.

Cumberland rum nicky

SERVES 6–8
●●●●●●●●●

For the sweet shortcrust
200g plain flour

2 tbsp icing sugar

100g cold unsalted butter,
cut into roughly 1cm dice

1 medium egg, lightly beaten

1 tsp lemon juice

2 tbsp very cold water

For the filling
225g dates, coarsely chopped

100g dried apricots, coarsely
chopped

50g stem ginger in syrup,
drained and finely chopped

50ml dark rum

50g soft dark brown sugar

50g unsalted butter, cut into
1–2cm cubes

For the rum butter
100g unsalted butter, softened

225g soft light brown sugar

75ml dark rum

Equipment
20cm metal pie plate, about
3cm deep

This traditional northern treat is a real favourite of mine. It's stuffed with sticky dates and treacly brown sugar and laced with ginger and rum – ingredients that came to Cumberland via the merchant ships that docked along the coastline. The name may stem from the original technique of covering the filling with a whole piece of pastry then making slashes or 'nicks' in it.

Start by mixing all the filling ingredients, except the butter, together in a bowl. Set aside to soak while you make the pastry.

For the pastry, mix the flour and icing sugar together in a bowl. Add the diced butter and rub it in with your fingertips until the mixture looks like fine breadcrumbs. Alternatively, do this in a food processor or a mixer and then transfer to a bowl.

Mix the egg with the lemon juice and water. Make a well in the centre of the flour mixture and pour in the egg mix. Using one hand, work the liquid into the flour to bring the pastry together. If it seems too dry, add a splash more water. When the dough begins to stick together, gently knead it into a ball. Wrap in cling film and rest in the fridge for at least 15 minutes.

Heat your oven to 180°C/gas 4 and have ready a 20cm metal pie plate, about 3cm deep.

Once the dough has rested, cut it into two pieces, roughly one-third and two-thirds. Roll out the larger piece on a lightly floured surface and use to line the pie dish, leaving the excess pastry hanging over the edge. Spread the filling in the pastry case and dot with the butter.

Roll out the remaining pastry and cut into 12–14 long strips, about 1cm wide. On a board covered with a sheet of parchment, use the pastry strips to create a lattice with 6–7 strips going each way, passing them under and over each other. Dampen the rim of the pastry in the tin with water then invert the lattice from the paper onto the tart. Press the ends of the strips to the pastry rim to secure and crimp the edges.

Bake for 15 minutes, then turn the oven down to 160°C/gas 3 and cook for a further 20 minutes. Meanwhile, for the rum butter, beat together the butter and sugar, then gradually beat in the rum.

Serve the tart warm or cold, with a spoonful of rum butter.

Step photographs overleaf

Cumberland rum nicky

Spooning the dried fruit filling into the pastry-lined pie plate.

Dotting the butter over the filling.

Rolling out the remaining pastry for the lattice top.

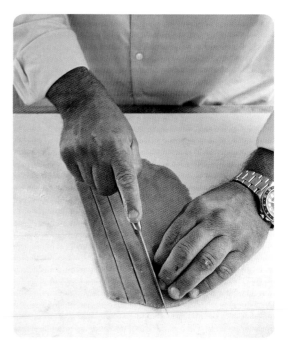

Cutting the pastry into strips for the lattice.

Weaving the strips of pastry on a piece of baking parchment to form a neat lattice.

The finished lattice, ready to go on the pie.

Inverting the lattice on top of the pie.

The finished pie, with the lattice neatly trimmed and the pastry edge crimped, ready to bake.

Sweet beetroot pie

●●●●●●●●●●

For the sweet shortcrust

200g plain flour

2 tbsp icing sugar

100g cold unsalted butter,
cut into roughly 1cm dice

1 medium egg, lightly beaten

1 tsp lemon juice

2 tbsp very cold water

For the filling

350g cooked peeled beetroot
(vacuum-packed is fine, but not
beetroot in vinegar)

125ml double cream

2 large eggs

175g dark muscovado sugar

1 tsp ground cinnamon

½ tsp ground ginger

Finely grated zest of 1 lemon

Equipment

23cm loose-based tart tin,
3cm deep

This recipe is based on the sweet, spicy American pumpkin pie but uses very British beetroot, which gives it an amazing, deep colour and flavour.

For the pastry, mix the flour and icing sugar together in a bowl. Add the diced butter and rub it in with your fingertips until the mixture looks like fine breadcrumbs. Alternatively, do this in a food processor or a mixer and then transfer to a bowl.

Mix the egg with the lemon juice and water. Make a well in the centre of the flour mixture and pour in the egg mix. Using one hand, work the liquid into the flour to bring the pastry together. If it seems too dry, add a splash more water. When the dough begins to stick together, gently knead it into a ball. Wrap in cling film and rest in the fridge for at least 15 minutes.

Heat your oven to 200°C/gas 6 and have ready a 23cm loose-based tart tin, 3cm deep.

Roll out the pastry on a lightly floured surface to about a 3mm thickness and use it to line the tart tin, leaving excess pastry hanging over the edge. Keep a little uncooked pastry back in case you need to patch any cracks later. Prick the base with a fork.

Line the pastry case with baking parchment or foil, then fill with baking beans, or uncooked rice or lentils. Bake blind for 15 minutes, then remove the parchment and baking beans and return to the oven for about 8 minutes or until the pastry looks dry and faintly coloured. Using a small, sharp knife, trim away the excess pastry from the edge. Use a tiny bit of the reserved raw pastry to patch any cracks or holes if necessary.

Turn the oven down to 180°C/gas 4.

For the filling, if you're using pre-packed beetroot, drain off any excess liquid, then roughly chop the beetroot and put into a food processor with the cream. Blend to a thick purée.

Whisk the eggs and sugar together thoroughly. Add the beetroot purée, spices and lemon zest and mix well.

Pour the mixture into the pastry case and bake for 30–40 minutes until the filling is set with a slight wobble in the middle. Leave to cool completely before serving, with crème fraîche.

Treacle tart

SERVES 6

●●●●●●●

For the sweet shortcrust

150g plain flour

2 tbsp icing sugar

75g cold unsalted butter,
cut into roughly 1cm dice

1 egg yolk

½ tsp lemon juice

1 tbsp very cold water

For the filling

350g golden syrup

50g unsalted butter, melted

3 tbsp double cream

1 large egg

Pinch of salt

125g slightly stale white
breadcrumbs

Finely grated zest of 1 lemon

Equipment

20cm loose-based cake tin,
4cm deep

Gloriously sweet but nicely cut with a little lemon acidity, a treacle tart is a wonderful, simple treat. You might think that it ought really to be called a syrup tart, since that's what it's based on – but 'golden syrup' was originally a trade name for what was also known as 'pale treacle'.

For the pastry, mix the flour and icing sugar together in a bowl. Add the diced butter and rub it in with your fingertips until the mixture looks like fine breadcrumbs. Alternatively, do this in a food processor or a mixer and then transfer to a bowl.

Mix the egg yolk with the lemon juice and water. Make a well in the centre of the flour mixture and pour in the egg mix. Using one hand, work the liquid into the flour to bring the pastry together. If it seems too dry, add a splash more water. When the dough begins to stick together, gently knead it into a ball. Wrap in cling film and rest in the fridge for at least 15 minutes.

Heat your oven to 200°C/gas 6 and have ready a 20cm loose-based cake tin, 4cm deep.

Roll out the pastry on a lightly floured surface and use to line the cake tin, leaving excess pastry hanging over the edge. Keep a little uncooked pastry back in case you need to patch any cracks later. Prick the base with a fork.

Line the pastry with baking parchment or foil, then fill with baking beans, or uncooked rice or lentils. Bake blind for 15 minutes, then remove the parchment and baking beans and return to the oven for about 8 minutes or until it looks dry and faintly coloured. Use a small, sharp knife to trim away the excess pastry from the edge of the tin. If necessary, patch any cracks or holes with raw pastry. Turn the oven down to 160°C/gas 3.

To make the filling, put the golden syrup into a saucepan and warm gently over a low heat to make it more liquid. Take off the heat and stir in the melted butter. Beat the cream with the egg and mix into the syrup. Add the salt, breadcrumbs and lemon zest and stir until combined. Pour into the pastry case.

Bake for 40–45 minutes or until the filling is coloured and just set. Remove from the oven and leave to cool completely in the tin. Slice and serve with whipped or clotted cream.

Gypsy tart

SERVES 6

●●●●●●●

For the sweet shortcrust

150g plain flour

2 tbsp icing sugar

75g cold unsalted butter,
cut into roughly 1cm dice

1 egg yolk

½ tsp lemon juice

1 tbsp very cold water

For the filling

230ml condensed milk

170g tin evaporated milk

175g light muscovado sugar

Equipment

20cm loose-based tart tin,
about 4.5cm deep

Muscovado sugar lends a rich caramel flavour to this unique, very sweet tart. The recipe comes from Kent but its history is uncertain. The story goes that the tart was first cooked by a kindly Kentish woman to feed some hungry gypsy children.

To make the pastry, mix the flour and icing sugar together in a bowl. Add the diced butter and rub it in with your fingertips until the mixture looks like fine breadcrumbs. Alternatively, do this in a food processor or a mixer and then transfer to a bowl.

Mix the egg yolk with the lemon juice and water. Make a well in the centre of the flour mixture and pour in the egg mix. Using one hand, work the liquid into the flour to bring the pastry together. If it seems too dry, add a splash more water. When the dough begins to stick together, gently knead it into a ball. Wrap in cling film and rest in the fridge for at least 15 minutes.

Heat your oven to 200°C/gas 6 and have ready a 20cm loose-based tart tin, about 4.5cm deep.

Roll out the pastry on a lightly floured surface to about a 3mm thickness and use it to line the tart tin, leaving excess pastry hanging over the edge. Keep a little uncooked pastry back in case you need to patch any cracks later. Prick the base with a fork.

Line the pastry case with baking parchment or foil, then fill with baking beans, or uncooked rice or lentils. Bake blind for 15 minutes, then remove the parchment and baking beans and return the pastry to the oven for about 8 minutes or until it looks dry and faintly coloured. Using a small, sharp knife, trim away the excess pastry from the edge. Use a tiny bit of the reserved raw pastry to patch any cracks or holes if necessary. Turn the oven down to 190°C/gas 5.

For the filling, put both milks and the sugar in a large bowl or the bowl of a mixer. Beat together with an electric whisk, starting off slowly then increasing the speed, for around 10 minutes until the mixture is increased in volume, light and bubbly.

Pour the mixture into the pastry case. Bake for about 20 minutes, until just set and still a bit wobbly in the centre. Remove from the oven and leave to cool in the tin before slicing and serving. A little crème fraîche or plain yoghurt balances the sweetness nicely.

Pecan pie

SERVES 6–8
●●●●●●●●●●

For the sweet shortcrust
200g plain flour

2 tbsp icing sugar

100g cold unsalted butter,
cut into roughly 1cm dice

1 medium egg, lightly beaten

1 tsp lemon juice

2 tbsp very cold water

For the filling
100g unsalted butter

150g golden syrup

125g dark muscovado sugar

200g pecan halves

3 medium eggs, beaten

Equipment
23cm loose-based tart tin,
3.5cm deep

I like this classic American recipe – it's very simple and really makes the most of the delicious affinity between nuts and toffee. The rich, dark, sticky filling is perfectly set off by a spoonful of lightly whipped cream.

To make the pastry, mix the flour and icing sugar together in a bowl. Add the diced butter and rub it in with your fingertips until the mixture looks like fine breadcrumbs. Alternatively, do this in a food processor or a mixer and then transfer to a bowl.

Mix the egg with the lemon juice and water. Make a well in the centre of the flour mixture and pour in the egg mix. Using one hand, work the liquid into the flour to bring the pastry together. If it seems too dry, add a splash more water. When the dough begins to stick together, gently knead it into a ball. Wrap in cling film and rest in the fridge for at least 15 minutes.

Heat your oven to 180°C/gas 4 and put in a baking tray to heat up. Have ready a 23cm loose-based tart tin, 3.5cm deep.

Roll out the pastry on a lightly floured surface and use it to line the tin. Prick the base with a fork. Put it in the fridge while you make the filling.

Put the butter, syrup and sugar in a saucepan and melt gently over a low heat. Once the butter has melted, remove from the heat and leave to cool for 10 minutes.

Arrange the pecans over the base of the pastry case. Mix the beaten eggs into the cooled syrup mixture and pour over the pecans.

Bake for 35–40 minutes or until the filling is almost set but still a bit wobbly. It will firm up as it cools. Leave to cool completely in the tin before serving, with whipped cream.

Individual fruit pies

●●●●●●●●●

For the sweet shortcrust

200g plain flour

2 tbsp icing sugar

100g cold unsalted butter,
cut into roughly 1cm dice

1 medium egg, lightly beaten

1 tsp lemon juice

2 tbsp very cold water

For the apple filling

7 medium eating apples (1kg)

25g unsalted butter

75g caster sugar

Finely grated zest of 1 lemon

50ml Calvados

2 tbsp mascarpone

For the pear filling

7 medium pears (about 1kg)

25g unsalted butter

75g caster sugar

Finely grated zest of 1 lemon

50ml perry

2 tbsp mascarpone

For the apricot filling

9 apricots (about 500g)

25g unsalted butter

75g caster sugar

50ml Amaretto

To finish

Beaten egg or milk for brushing

Granulated sugar for sprinkling

Equipment

12-hole bun tray

8.5cm, 6cm and 6.5–7cm cutters

With their luscious fruity filling, these little pies remind me of the ones my Nan used to make. They are a real treat, especially when served warm with whipped cream. I've given you three fillings to choose from; each uses the full quantity of pastry.

To make the pastry, mix the flour and icing sugar together in a bowl. Add the diced butter and rub it in with your fingertips until the mixture looks like fine breadcrumbs. Alternatively, do this in a food processor or a mixer and then transfer to a bowl.

Mix the egg with the lemon juice and water. Make a well in the centre of the flour mixture and pour in the egg mix. Using one hand, work the liquid into the flour to bring the pastry together. If it seems too dry, add a splash more water. When the dough begins to stick together, gently knead it into a ball. Wrap in cling film and rest in the fridge for at least 15 minutes.

To make any of the fillings, first prepare the fruit. Peel, quarter and core apples or pears; halve and stone apricots. Cut the fruit into 1cm pieces. Melt the butter in a wide pan over a medium heat. Add the fruit, sugar, lemon zest (if applicable) and the alcohol. Simmer for about 10 minutes, stirring from time to time, until the fruit is tender and most of the liquid has evaporated. Leave to cool completely, then mix in the mascarpone (if included) and chill the mixture.

Heat your oven to 200°C/gas 6.

On a lightly floured surface, roll out the pastry until 2–3mm thick. Using an 8.5cm plain cutter, cut out 12 circles and use them to line a bun tray (the kind you use for fairy cakes, not a deep muffin tray). Re-roll the pastry as necessary and cut out 6cm circles, for the lids.

Spoon the filling into the pastry cases, taking care not to overfill them. Dampen the rim of the pastry with water and top each pie with a lid. Press a 6.5–7cm cutter over the pie to seal the edge and trim away any excess pastry. Make a small steam hole in the top of each pie. Brush with a little beaten egg or milk and sprinkle with sugar. Bake for 25–30 minutes until the pastry is crisp and golden.

Leave to cool in the tin for 5 minutes before removing. Serve warm or at room temperature, within 24 hours of baking, or they'll start to lose their crispness.

Step photographs overleaf

Individual fruit pies

Using an 8.5cm cutter to stamp out circles from the pastry.

Lining a 12-hole bun tin with the circles, pressing the pastry well into the corners.

Spooning the apple filling into the pastry cases.

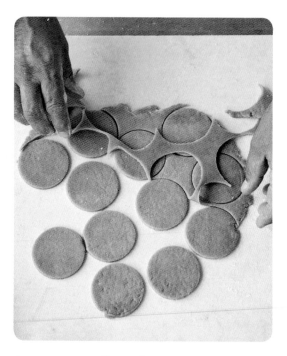

Cutting out smaller circles, 6cm in diameter, for the lids.

Positioning the pastry lids.

Pressing a smaller cutter over the pie to seal the edge and trim away excess pastry.

Brushing the tops of the pies with beaten egg.

The sugar-dusted pies, ready for the oven.

Chocolate & prune tart

SERVES 6
●●●●●●●

For the chocolate pastry

175g plain flour
2 tbsp icing sugar
2 tbsp cocoa powder
100g cold unsalted butter,
cut into roughly 1cm dice
1 egg yolk
1 tsp lemon juice
2 tbsp very cold water

For the filling

150g ready-to-eat prunes
(ideally d'Agen), cut into
quarters
1 tbsp brandy
1 tsp vanilla extract
50ml boiling water
75g dark chocolate, broken
into small pieces
125ml double cream
200g mascarpone
2 medium eggs, beaten

Equipment

23cm loose-based tart tin,
3.5cm deep

The combination of prunes, chocolate and brandy rarely fails to please and this deliciously dark and sophisticated tart uses cocoa pastry for an extra chocolate hit.

For the filling, put the prunes, brandy and vanilla in a bowl. Pour on the boiling water and leave to soak for several hours or overnight.

To make the pastry, sift the flour, icing sugar and cocoa together. Add the diced butter and rub it in with your fingertips until the mixture looks like fine breadcrumbs. Alternatively, do this in a food processor or a mixer and then transfer to a bowl.

Mix the egg yolk with the lemon juice and water. Make a well in the centre of the flour mixture and pour in the egg mix. Using one hand, work the liquid into the flour to bring the pastry together. If it seems too dry, add a splash more water. When the dough begins to stick together, gently knead it into a ball. Wrap the pastry in cling film and put in the fridge to rest for at least 15 minutes.

Heat your oven to 200°C/gas 6.

Roll out the pastry on a lightly floured surface and use to line a 23cm loose-based tart tin, 3.5cm deep, leaving excess pastry hanging over the edge. Keep a little uncooked pastry back in case you need to patch any cracks later. Prick the base with a fork.

Line the pastry with baking parchment or foil, then fill with baking beans, or uncooked rice or lentils. Bake blind for 15 minutes, then remove the parchment and baking beans and return to the oven for about 8 minutes or until the pastry looks dry. Use a small, sharp knife to trim away the excess pastry from the edge. Use a tiny bit of the reserved raw pastry to patch any cracks or holes if necessary. Turn the oven down to 180°C/gas 4.

To make the filling, put the chocolate and cream in a heatproof bowl over a pan of simmering water and leave until the chocolate has just melted, stirring from time to time. Take off the heat and leave to cool for 3 minutes, then beat in the mascarpone and eggs with a balloon whisk to keep it smooth. Stir in the prunes and any soaking juices.

Pour the chocolate and prune mixture into the tart case. Bake for 20–25 minutes until almost set, with a bit of wobble still in the centre. Leave in the tin to cool completely. Serve the tart at room temperature, with a spoonful of cream if you like.

Spiced plum pizza

SERVES 6–8

●●●●●●●●●

For the pizza dough
250g strong white bread flour

5g fine salt

20g caster sugar

5g fast-action dried yeast

30g unsalted butter, cut into
small cubes

180ml water

For the plum topping
100g dark muscovado sugar

1 tsp ground cinnamon

1 tsp ground star anise

Finely grated zest of 1 orange

2 tbsp semolina

1kg firm, slightly under-ripe
plums, stoned and halved,
or quartered if large

15g unsalted butter, cut into
small pieces

Equipment
30cm pizza pan or tart tin,
about 2cm deep

With its generous filling encased in a lightly sweetened and enriched dough, this gorgeous fruit pizza makes an impressive centrepiece. Make it in August or September when our plums are at their juicy best.

To make the pizza dough, put the flour in a bowl and add the salt and sugar to one side and the yeast to the other. Combine them, then add the butter and rub it into the flour with your fingertips. Add 150ml of the water and start mixing with your fingers, gradually incorporating all the flour from the edges of the bowl, and adding more water a little at a time, until you have a rough dough. You may not need to add all the water (or you may need a little more) but the dough should be very soft and sticky.

Tip the dough out onto a lightly floured surface and knead it for 5–10 minutes until it is smooth and elastic. Shape into a ball and place in a lightly oiled bowl. Cover and leave in a fairly warm place for about 1½ hours until tripled in size.

Heat your oven to 220°C/gas 7. Have ready a 30cm pizza pan or a similar-sized tart tin, about 2cm deep.

Shortly before you're ready to bake the pizza, for the topping, mix the muscovado sugar, cinnamon, star anise and orange zest together in a large bowl.

Tip the risen dough onto a lightly floured work surface. Gently knock the air out of the dough, then roll it out to a circle, about 35cm in diameter. Lift the dough into the pizza pan and press well into the corners of the tin and onto the base, leaving the excess dough hanging over the edge. Sprinkle the semolina over the base.

Scatter the plums into the lined pizza pan, sprinkle with the spiced sugar mixture and dot with the butter.

Bake for 30 minutes, until the dough is a dark golden colour and the plums are tender but still holding their shape. Leave to cool slightly for 5 minutes before serving on a large wooden board dusted with icing sugar.

Step photographs overleaf

Spiced plum pizza

Kneading the pizza dough on a lightly floured surface until smooth and elastic.

Shaping the dough into a ball, ready to place in a bowl and leave in a warm place to rise.

The risen pizza dough, ready to pummel and knock back.

Rolling out the dough on a lightly floured surface to a large round.

Carefully lifting the thinly rolled dough into the pizza pan.

Pressing the dough into the corners of the pan.

Pressing the dough onto the base of the pan.

Sprinkling the spiced sugar mixture over the plums in the pizza case.

Chocolate orange pond pudding

SERVES 4–6

●●●●●●●●●

150g unsalted butter, cut into
1–2cm cubes, plus extra for
greasing

185g self-raising flour

15g cocoa powder

20g caster sugar

125g shredded suet

1 orange

150–175ml whole milk

150g soft dark brown sugar

25g dark chocolate, chopped
into small pieces

Equipment

1.2 litre pudding basin

This is my take on Sussex pond pudding – the classic suet pud boiled with a whole lemon inside. I use a whole orange instead and add chocolate. The juice from the fruit combines with the melted chocolate, butter and sugar to create an irresistible sauce that floods out as the pudding is cut – hence the name.

Grease a 1.2 litre pudding basin with butter.

Mix the flour, cocoa, caster sugar and suet together in a large bowl. Finely grate the zest of the orange and mix this in too. Gradually work in enough milk to form a soft, slightly sticky dough.

Take a third of the pastry. Roll out on a lightly floured surface to a circle slightly bigger than the basin. Invert the basin onto the pastry and cut around it to form a lid. Add the offcuts to the remaining pastry and roll out to a circle, about 30cm in diameter. Use this to line the pudding basin. Make sure there are no cracks in the pastry.

Put half the butter, brown sugar and chocolate in the lined basin. Pierce the zested orange all over with a skewer and sit it on top. Add the remaining butter, sugar and chocolate.

Dampen the pastry edges with milk or water and put the pastry lid on top. Press the edges together to seal and trim off the excess.

Place a piece of baking parchment on a sheet of foil and make a large pleat in the middle, folding both sheets together. Put the parchment and foil on top of the pudding, foil side up, and secure with string, looping the end of the string over the top of the pudding and tying it to form a handle (as shown on page 91).

Stand the pudding basin in a large pan and pour in enough boiling water to come halfway up the side of the basin. Put a tight-fitting lid on the pan and bring to a simmer. Lower the heat to maintain a simmer and steam the pudding for 2¼ hours. Top up the boiling water during this time if necessary so the pan doesn't boil dry.

Lift the pudding basin from the pan. Remove the paper and foil and run the tip of a small, sharp knife around the edge of the pudding, to help release it, if necessary. Invert a large plate or deep dish over the top of the basin and turn both over to unmould the pudding.

Serve at once, cutting into the pudding carefully as the juices flood out (the orange isn't intended to be eaten). Serve with cold cream.

Gooseberry & elderflower crumble

SERVES 4–6

●●●●●●●●●

For the filling
500g fresh gooseberries,
topped and tailed
1 large cooking apple (about
225g), peeled, cored and diced
50ml elderflower cordial
100g soft light brown sugar

For the crumble topping
100g plain wholemeal flour
75g porridge oats
100g soft dark brown sugar
75g cold unsalted butter,
cut into roughly 1cm dice
25g sunflower seeds
15g pumpkin seeds

Equipment
25 x 20cm baking dish

Gooseberry and elderflower is a classic combination, but this crumble is a little different to most. I make the topping with wholemeal flour, brown sugar and crushed seeds, to give it extra colour and flavour.

Heat your oven to 180°C/gas 4 and have ready a baking dish, about 25 x 20cm.

To make the filling, put the gooseberries, apple, elderflower cordial and sugar in a pan. Cook over a medium heat for about 10 minutes, stirring from time to time, until the sugar has dissolved and the fruit is just beginning to collapse. Taste and add more sugar if required then transfer the mixture to the baking dish and set aside.

To make the crumble topping, combine the flour, oats and sugar in a bowl. Add the butter and rub in lightly with your fingertips until the mixture resembles coarse crumbs.

Using a pestle and mortar or a small processor, crush the sunflower and pumpkin seeds so they break down a little. Do not reduce them to a fine powder. Stir the crushed seeds into the crumble mixture.

Spoon the crumble mixture over the gooseberry filling. Bake for 35–40 minutes until golden brown and bubbling. Leave to settle for about 10 minutes, then serve with custard, cream or ice cream.

Apricot, peach & almond cobbler

SERVES 6
●●●●●●●

For the filling
350g apricots

350g peaches

3 tbsp honey

75g good-quality ready-made
marzipan, chilled

For the cobbler topping
175g plain flour

2½ tsp baking powder

2 tbsp caster sugar

75g cold unsalted butter,
cut into roughly 1cm dice

125ml single cream

1 egg white

2 tbsp demerara sugar

Equipment

1.3 litre ovenproof dish

With its scrumptious, golden scone-like topping, a cobbler lies somewhere between a crumble and a pie. You can use all sorts of fruit, depending on what's in season – this recipe is ideal for late summer. The almond element comes from sweet marzipan, which is grated onto the fruit, enhancing the apricots and peaches beautifully.

Heat your oven to 190°C/gas 5.

For the filling, cut the apricots and peaches into quarters and prise out the stones. Cut the peach quarters in two if they are large. Combine the fruit in a 1.3 litre ovenproof dish. Drizzle over the honey, then coarsely grate the marzipan over the fruit.

To make the cobbler dough, put the flour, baking powder and caster sugar into a large bowl and mix well. Add the butter and rub it in lightly with your fingers until the mixture resembles breadcrumbs. Stir in the cream, a little at a time, bringing the mixture together into a soft dough; you may not need all the cream.

With floured hands, divide the cobbler mixture into 10 pieces. Roll each portion into a ball and flatten slightly with the heel of your hand to make a 'cobble'. Carefully place the cobbles on top of the fruit and marzipan.

Brush the cobbles with egg white and sprinkle with demerara sugar. Bake the cobbler for 40 minutes or until the topping is risen and golden brown and the fruit is bubbling. Serve warm, with cream.

Apple & blackberry charlottes

SERVES 4

●●●●●●●

125g unsalted butter

500g cooking apples, peeled, cored and chopped

75g caster sugar

250g blackberries

About 400g slightly stale white bread, cut into 7–8mm slices, crusts removed

Equipment

4 individual pudding moulds, 175ml capacity

In these puddings, crisp, buttery bread takes the place of pastry. Apple is the classic filling, and recipes for apple charlottes date back over 200 years, but adding blackberries makes them all the more delicious. No one knows exactly how the name came about but it is often thought to be a tribute to Queen Charlotte, wife of George III.

Heat your oven to 200°C/gas 6.

Melt 25g of the butter in a large saucepan. Add the apples and sugar and cook gently for about 5 minutes, until the apples begin to soften, but are not cooked through. You may need to add a splash of water. Remove the apples from the heat. Stir in the blackberries, then taste for sweetness and add more sugar if required. The filling should be quite sweet as there is no sugar in the bread cases.

Melt the remaining butter and use some of it to grease 4 individual pudding moulds, 175ml capacity.

Cut 4 bread discs to fit in the bases of the moulds and 4 larger discs to fit the tops. Cut the remaining bread into 3–4cm strips. Brush one side of each piece of bread with melted butter. Put the smaller discs in the base of the moulds, butter side down. Line the sides with the bread strips, butter side outwards. Cut extra pieces of bread to fill any gaps so the bread lining is snug.

Divide the apple and blackberry filling between the lined moulds. Top with the bread lids. Fold any excess bread from the sides over the lid to help keep it in place.

Stand the pudding moulds on a baking tray and bake in the oven for 30–35 minutes until the bread is golden brown. Leave to stand for 5–10 minutes, then turn out into shallow bowls and serve warm, with ice cream or custard.

Step photographs overleaf

Apple & blackberry charlottes

Lining the sides of the moulds with the bread strips, butter side outwards.

Spooning the fruit filling into the bread-lined moulds.

Cutting out bread discs to fit the tops of the moulds.

Positioning the bread lids over the filling.

Folding the ends of the bread strips over the top
of the pastry lid and pressing down gently.

Chocolate bread & butter pudding

SERVES 6
●●●●●●●

25g unsalted butter, softened
About 500g come-again cake (see page 210) or other leftover cake
50g sultanas
100ml whole milk
325ml double cream
150g dark chocolate, finely chopped
2 large eggs
25g caster sugar
1 tbsp demerara sugar

Equipment
18 x 23cm ovenproof dish

I've given a twist to this classic dish by using cake instead of leftover bread. My come-again cake on page 210 works a treat (you'll need about two-thirds of it), but any decent cake will do.

Use the butter to grease an ovenproof dish, about 18 x 23cm.

Cut the cake into roughly 1.5cm slices and cut each into quarters. Arrange one-third of the cake slices in the buttered dish. Sprinkle over one-third of the sultanas. Repeat twice, using up all the cake and sultanas.

In a saucepan, heat the milk and cream until almost boiling. Take off the heat and tip in the chopped chocolate. Whisk until all the chocolate has melted. You can heat the mixture gently again if you need to, to get it completely smooth, but don't let it boil.

Whisk the eggs and caster sugar together in a large bowl or jug. Gradually pour on the chocolate cream, whisking until all the cream is incorporated and you have a smooth chocolate custard.

Pour the custard over the cake in the dish then leave to stand for 30 minutes so the cake can absorb some of the custard.

Heat your oven to 180°C/gas 4.

Sprinkle the demerara sugar over the surface of the pudding and bake for 30–40 minutes, until the custard has set. Leave to stand for 15 minutes or so before serving, with cold cream.

Cherry croissant pudding

SERVES 6

● ● ● ● ● ● ● ●

Butter for greasing

300ml double cream

300ml whole milk

75g caster sugar

4 large egg yolks

2 tbsp Kirsch

6 medium or 4 large croissants

5–6 tbsp cherry conserve
or jam

100g cherries, stoned and
halved

Equipment

1.2 litre ovenproof dish

This takes the classic bread and butter pud idea and raises it to new heights. The croissants soak up the Kirsch-scented custard beautifully, but go deliciously crisp on top.

Grease a 1.2 litre ovenproof dish.

Pour the cream and milk into a saucepan and heat just to the boil, then remove from the heat. Beat the sugar and egg yolks together in a large bowl, then pour on the hot milk and beat thoroughly. Stir in the Kirsch.

Halve each croissant and spread with the cherry conserve. Arrange in the ovenproof dish. Scatter over the cherries and pour over the custard. Leave to stand for about 30 minutes to allow the custard to soak into the croissants.

Meanwhile, heat your oven to 160°C/gas 3. Bake the pudding for 40–45 minutes, until the custard is set. If the top seems to be browning too quickly, cover the pudding with foil. Serve warm.

Queen of puddings

SERVES 4
●●●●●●●●

For the puddings

Butter for greasing

75g slightly stale white
breadcrumbs

100g raspberry jam

For the custard

600ml whole milk

1 vanilla pod

50g caster sugar

1 large egg

2 large egg yolks

For the meringue topping

4 large egg whites

150g caster sugar

Equipment

4 individual heatproof dishes,
about 10cm in diameter

Roasting tray

**This nursery pud is a classic, and a great way to turn some
leftover slices of bread and a few storecupboard staples into
a spectacular little treat.**

Heat your oven to 180°C/gas 4. Butter 4 individual heatproof glass
dishes, about 10cm in diameter. Divide the breadcrumbs between
them, scattering them evenly.

To make the custard, pour the milk into a saucepan. Split open the
vanilla pod with a small, sharp knife and scrape out the seeds with
the tip of the knife. Add both the seeds and the pod to the saucepan.
Slowly bring the milk just to the boil, then take off the heat.

Whisk the sugar, egg and egg yolks together in a bowl. Pour on the
hot milk and whisk well. Strain this back into the pan or into a jug.

Pour the custard into the prepared dishes, dividing it equally.

Stand the dishes in a roasting tray and pour in enough hot water
to come about halfway up the sides of the dishes. Bake in the oven
for 25–30 minutes, or until the custards are set. Remove the dishes
from the roasting tray and allow to cool.

If your jam is very stiff, beat it to soften, or heat it slightly. When
the custards are cool, spread the jam over them. Return the dishes
to the emptied-out roasting tin.

For the meringue topping, whisk the egg whites with an electric
whisk, or using a mixer with a whisk attachment, until they hold
stiff peaks. Whisk in the sugar a spoonful at a time, until you have
a fluffy meringue that holds stiff peaks.

Spoon the meringue into a piping bag fitted with a 1cm nozzle and
pipe it on top of the jam-topped custards, or simply spoon it on top
and swirl decoratively. Bake for 10–15 minutes, until the meringue
is golden, then serve straight away.

Step photographs overleaf

Queen of puddings

Whisking the sugar, egg and egg yolks together for the custard.

Whisking the vanilla-infused hot milk into the egg and sugar mixture.

Pouring the warm custard over the breadcrumbs in the dishes.

Pouring hot water into the roasting tray to make a bain marie for the custards to gently cook in.

Spooning the raspberry jam on top of the cooled custards.

Whisking the egg whites for the meringue until forming stiff peaks.

Whisking the sugar into the whisked egg whites to make a stiff, glossy meringue.

Piping the meringue onto the jam-topped custards, ready to bake.

Steamed liquorice sponges

SERVES 4
●●●●●●●

100g unsalted butter, softened,
plus extra for greasing
4 liquorice spirals
or Pontefract cakes
100g caster sugar
3 medium eggs
100g self-raising flour
1 tsp baking powder
1 tsp liquorice extract

Equipment

4 dariole moulds or
individual pudding moulds,
175ml capacity

With these light and fluffy puddings, I've created a dish that carries the memory of some of the sweet-shop flavours of my childhood. Liquorice was the obvious choice – it has a lovely fruity tang that enhances the sponge beautifully.

Butter 4 dariole moulds or individual pudding basins, about 175ml capacity, and line the base of each with a disc of baking parchment.

Place a liquorice spiral or Pontefract cake in the base of each prepared mould.

Put all the remaining ingredients in a large bowl and beat together using an electric whisk. Start off slowly, then increase the speed and mix for 2 minutes until all the ingredients are well combined.

Divide the mixture between the moulds. Tap each mould on the work surface to remove any air pockets and level out the mixture.

Create a lid for each pudding by placing a small piece of baking parchment over a small piece of foil and making a pleat in the middle, folding both sheets together (to allow for the puddings' expansion as they cook). Put the lids on top of the pudding moulds, foil side up, and secure with string.

Stand the moulds in a steamer. Alternatively, put them in a large saucepan and pour in enough boiling water to come halfway up the sides of the moulds. Put the lid on the pan and bring to a simmer. Either way, steam the puddings for 45 minutes.

Uncover the puddings and run the tip of a small, sharp knife around the edge of each, to help release them. Invert them onto warmed plates and serve straight away, with custard.

Heather honey sponge

SERVES 4
●●●●●●●

100g unsalted butter, softened,
plus extra for greasing
130g heather honey
100g caster sugar
3 medium eggs
110g self-raising flour
1 tsp baking powder

Equipment
1 litre pudding basin

There's nothing to compare to the light, fluffy texture of a steamed sponge pudding. Golden syrup is a classic addition, of course, but I love this version, which makes the most of the fragrant flavour of Scottish heather honey. Any other well-flavoured honey will work too.

Butter a 1 litre pudding basin. Put 2 tbsp of the honey into the prepared basin (if the honey is very thick, warm it gently first to make it more liquid).

Put the remaining honey and all the other ingredients into a large bowl and beat together using an electric whisk. Start off slowly, then increase the speed and mix for 2 minutes until all the ingredients are well combined.

Spoon the mixture into the pudding basin, on top of the honey.

Place a piece of baking parchment on a sheet of foil and make a large pleat in the middle, folding both sheets together (this allows for the pudding's expansion as it cooks). Put the parchment and foil on top of the pudding, foil side up, and secure with string, looping the end of the string over the top of the pudding and tying it to form a handle that will enable you to lift the pudding in and out of the pan (as shown on page 91).

Stand the pudding basin in a large pan and pour in enough boiling water to come halfway up the side of the basin. Put a tight-fitting lid on the pan and bring to a simmer. Lower the heat to maintain a simmer and steam the pudding for 1¼ hours or until risen and springy to the touch. Top up the boiling water during this time if necessary so the pan doesn't boil dry.

Carefully lift the pudding basin from the pan, remove the foil and parchment and run the tip of a small, sharp knife around the edge of the pudding to help release it. Turn out onto a warmed large plate and serve piping hot, with custard or cream.

Sticky toffee pudding

●●●●●●●●●

For the pudding

75g unsalted butter, softened,
plus extra for greasing

175g stoned dates, chopped

200ml boiling water

1 tsp bicarbonate of soda

150g soft dark brown sugar

2 medium eggs, beaten

175g self-raising flour

½ tsp baking powder

2 tbsp fudge pieces

75g macadamia nuts, coarsely
chopped

For the sticky toffee sauce

100g unsalted butter,
cut into chunks

150g soft dark brown sugar

150ml double cream

Equipment

24 x 26cm baking tin,
4-5cm deep

Puddings don't get more gloriously indulgent than this one. Its origins are shrouded in mystery, but it is believed to have been invented at The Sharrow Bay Hotel in the Lake District in the seventies. I love the fact that it is not just about sweetness; there are lots of rich and nutty flavours in there too, making it the perfect pud after Sunday lunch on a cold winter's day.

Heat your oven to 180°C/gas 4 and butter a 24 x 26cm baking tin, 4-5cm deep.

Put the dates in a bowl, pour on the boiling water and stir in the bicarbonate of soda.

Cream the butter and sugar together in a large bowl until light and fluffy. Gradually add the beaten egg, beating well after each addition. Sift the flour and baking powder together over the mixture and fold in. Stir in the dates and their soaking water, then fold in the fudge pieces and 50g of the macadamia nuts.

Transfer the mixture to the prepared tin, spreading it evenly. Bake for 25-30 minutes, until firm and springy to the touch.

Meanwhile, to make the toffee sauce, melt together the butter, sugar and cream in a saucepan over a low heat. Bring to the boil and let bubble for 3-4 minutes, until the sauce is thick enough to coat the back of a wooden spoon.

Preheat your grill to high. Make holes all over the cooked pudding with a skewer. Pour half the sauce over the pudding and place under the hot grill. Grill for 2-3 minutes until the sauce is bubbling. Keep your eye on it as it can burn easily.

Cut the hot pudding into portions and serve with the remaining warm toffee sauce, sprinkled with the rest of the chopped nuts, and ice cream or cream.

Chocolate volcanoes

MAKES 4

●●●●●●●

165g unsalted butter, cut into small pieces, plus extra for greasing

165g dark chocolate, about 70% cocoa solids, chopped into small pieces

3 medium eggs

3 medium egg yolks

85g caster sugar

2 tbsp plain flour

Equipment

4 individual pudding moulds or dariole moulds, 175ml capacity

This is my version of the classic chocolate fondant – but I like this name better. These little hot chocolate puddings really do remind me of volcanoes as they release their soft, silky river of chocolate. Achieving the molten centre is all about timing. Don't let the puddings bake to the point that their surface begins to crack, as this means the centres are starting to cook.

Grease 4 individual pudding moulds, about 175ml capacity, with a little butter.

Put the butter and chocolate into a heatproof bowl over a pan of gently simmering water (bain marie). Remove the pan from the heat and leave to melt, stirring once or twice.

Using an electric whisk, whisk the eggs, egg yolks and sugar together for several minutes until thick, pale and moussey.

Carefully fold the chocolate mixture into the egg and sugar mix, using a spatula or large metal spoon. Sift in the flour and fold this in carefully too.

Divide the chocolate mixture between the prepared moulds. Place in the fridge for at least 2 hours until firm. (You can make the puddings up to 24 hours in advance and leave them in the fridge until you are ready to cook and serve them.)

When you are ready to cook, heat the oven to 200°C/gas 6. Stand the moulds on a baking tray and bake for 12–14 minutes, or until the puddings are risen but not cracked.

Turn the puddings out onto individual plates and serve at once, with pouring cream.

Step photographs overleaf

Chocolate volcanoes

Melting the butter and chocolate together, over a bain marie.

Whisking the eggs, egg yolks and sugar together, using a handheld electric whisk.

Whisked until pale and moussey, the egg and sugar mixture is thick enough to leave a trail.

Adding the melted chocolate mix to the whisked mixture and starting to fold it in with a spatula.

Continuing to fold the two mixtures together to combine evenly.

Carefully folding in the flour, using a cutting and folding action to avoid knocking out air.

Spooning the chocolate mixture into the prepared pudding moulds.

Standing the pudding moulds on a baking tray, ready to chill before baking.

Traditional rice pudding

SERVES 4

●●●●●●●●

60g pudding rice
600ml whole milk
1 tbsp skimmed milk powder
2 tbsp caster sugar
1 thinly pared strip of lemon zest
Freshly grated nutmeg, to taste
15g unsalted butter, cut into
small dice

Equipment
1 litre baking dish

An oldie but a goodie, this is one of the best and simplest of all puds. You just need to serve it with a blob of jam for sheer comfort food heaven. The little bit of milk powder in the mix is an old trick that makes the pudding especially creamy.

Heat your oven to 150°C/gas 2.

Wash the rice and drain in a sieve, then put it into a wide baking dish, at least 1 litre capacity. Pour on the milk. Add the milk powder, caster sugar and lemon zest and stir together. Grate some nutmeg over the top and dot with the butter.

Bake in the oven for 2–2½ hours, until the pudding has a golden brown skin and the rice is tender and creamy (the longer you give it, the thicker and stickier it will become).

Serve warm, with a blob of your favourite jam on top.

Coffee crème caramels

MAKES 4

●●●●●●●●

For the custard

1 tbsp instant coffee granules

75g caster sugar

600ml whole milk

3 medium eggs

3 medium egg yolks

For the caramel

125g caster sugar

50ml water

Equipment

4 ramekins or individual pudding moulds, 175ml capacity

Roasting tray

These are very sophisticated puds, the sweetness of the custard balancing the flavour of the coffee, with a touch of bitterness from the caramel. You need to make them a day in advance so they can sit in the fridge, where the caramel will gradually melt into the coffee custard.

Heat your oven to 150°C/gas 2. Have ready 4 ramekins or individual pudding moulds, about 175ml capacity.

For the custard, put the coffee, sugar and milk in a saucepan and bring slowly up to simmering point, stirring occasionally to dissolve the coffee. Do not boil. Remove from the heat and set aside while you make the caramel.

Put the sugar and water for the caramel in a heavy-based saucepan. Heat gently until the sugar has dissolved, then bring to the boil. Boil steadily for a few minutes until the syrup has turned to a dark golden caramel.

As soon as the caramel has reached the right colour, pour it into the moulds. Tilt and rotate the moulds to swirl the caramel and coat partway up the sides; take care because it will be extremely hot. Leave to set (but do not refrigerate) while you make the custard.

Beat the eggs and egg yolks together in a large bowl. Gently pour on the coffee-flavoured milk, whisking as you do so until well combined. Strain the custard into a jug, then pour into the moulds.

Stand the moulds in a roasting tray and pour enough hot water into the tray to come about three-quarters of the way up the sides of the moulds. Cover the tray with foil and place in the oven. Bake for 40–45 minutes, or until the custards are just set but still have a slight wobble.

Remove the moulds from the roasting tray and leave the custards to cool completely, then refrigerate for 24 hours.

To turn out the puddings, first run a thin-bladed knife around the outside of the custard, then invert a deep plate over the top and turn the mould and plate over, so the custard and its lovely caramel slide out onto the plate. Serve straight away.

Step photographs overleaf

Coffee crème caramels

Boiling the sugar syrup steadily to a dark golden caramel.

Carefully pouring the very hot caramel into the individual moulds.

Tilting and rotating the moulds to swirl the caramel partway up the sides.

Pouring the strained custard over the caramel in the moulds.

Pouring hot water into the roasting tray to make
a bain marie for the custards to gently cook in.

Lemon & lavender posset with lavender biscuits

SERVES 4–6

For the posset

600ml double cream

150g caster sugar

1 tbsp lavender (fresh buds and leaves or edible dried lavender)

Juice of 2 lemons, strained

For the lavender biscuits

100g unsalted butter, softened

2 tsp lavender (fresh buds and leaves or edible dried lavender)

50g caster sugar

175g plain flour

Equipment

4 glass tumblers or small dishes, or 6 espresso cups

A posset is a very simple pudding that dates back to the Middle Ages. It was originally made by adding lemon juice or wine to milk but modern versions rely on cream. Here I've used lemon juice and fragrant lavender to cut the richness of the cream. You can buy edible dried lavender from baking suppliers and some supermarkets. Alternatively, if you have lavender in your garden, you can use fresh buds and leaves, finely chopped.

To make the posset, put the cream, sugar and lavender in a pan. Slowly bring to the boil, stirring all the time to dissolve the sugar. Reduce the heat a little and simmer for 2–3 minutes, stirring often so the cream doesn't stick and burn.

Remove the pan from the heat and stir in the lemon juice. Leave to cool for 5 minutes, then pour into 4 glass tumblers or small dishes, or 6 espresso cups. Leave to cool completely then cover with cling film and chill in the fridge for at least 3 hours, until set. Remove from the fridge 20 minutes before serving.

To make the biscuits, beat the butter and lavender together in a bowl; this helps release the flavour of the lavender. Add the sugar and beat until pale and fluffy. Work in the flour with a fork or wooden spoon. Don't worry if it seems like there is too much flour at this point – it is supposed to be a fairly dry mix. Use your hands to bring the mixture together into a smooth dough.

Form the mixture into a cylinder, about 4cm in diameter and 18cm long, and wrap in greaseproof paper or cling film. Put in the fridge for at least a couple of hours, until firm.

When you are ready to bake the biscuits, heat your oven to 160°C/ gas 3 and line a large baking tray with baking parchment.

Unwrap the dough and use a sharp, serrated knife to cut 5mm thick discs from the cylinder. Place these discs on the lined tray, allowing room for the biscuits to spread a little. (You'll need to cook them in batches.) Bake for about 15 minutes, until the edges of the biscuits are just starting to turn golden. Transfer to a wire rack to cool.

Serve the lemon posset with the lavender biscuits. Any leftover biscuits will keep in an airtight container for a few days.

Baked custards with pistachio shards

SERVES 6
●●●●●●●

For the custards

1 vanilla pod

500ml double cream

100ml whole milk

6 large egg yolks

50g caster sugar

For the pistachio shards

75g unsalted, shelled
pistachio nuts

125g caster sugar

50ml water

Equipment

6 ramekins

Roasting tray

This is a variation on the classic crème brûlée, which normally calls for a super-thin, burnt-sugar topping. Getting that just right can be a bit tricky; making the caramel separately is a handy shortcut that many chefs use. I like to add some nuts to the caramel too, so you get a praline flavour to enhance the simple custard. This is a great pud to make in advance.

Heat your oven to 150°C/gas 2.

To make the custards, split the vanilla pod in half and scrape out the seeds with the tip of a small, sharp knife. Pour the cream and milk into a saucepan and add the vanilla seeds. Heat until just below boiling, then remove from the heat.

In a bowl, whisk the egg yolks and sugar together until thoroughly combined. Pour on the hot vanilla cream and whisk until smooth. Ladle into 6 ramekins.

Stand the ramekins in a roasting tray and pour in enough hot water to come halfway up the side of the dishes. Cover the tin with foil and bake for 30–40 minutes or until the custards are just set. There should be a slight wobble in the centre of the set custards.

Remove the ramekins from the roasting tray and allow to cool, then cover and put in the fridge to chill for about 3 hours.

To make the pistachio shards, first toast the pistachio nuts in a dry frying pan over a medium heat for a few minutes, until lightly coloured and fragrant. Tip them out onto a board and chop them roughly. Put to one side.

Lay a large piece of baking parchment on a baking tray. Put the sugar and water in a heavy-based pan. Heat gently until the sugar has dissolved, then bring to the boil and boil for a few minutes until the syrup has turned to a dark golden caramel. Immediately pour onto the lined baking tray and sprinkle with the pistachios. Leave the praline to set hard (not in the fridge).

If you are not serving straight away, put the pistachio praline in an airtight container as soon as it has set and cooled, to keep it crisp and brittle.

When you are ready to serve, break the praline into rough shards. Serve the chilled custards topped with the shards.

Hazelnut meringue roulade

SERVES 8
●●●●●●●●

For the meringue
4 medium egg whites
225g caster sugar
75g toasted, skinned hazelnuts,
finely chopped

For the filling
350ml double cream
3 tbsp chocolate hazelnut
spread
25g dark chocolate, finely
grated
25g toasted, skinned hazelnuts,
finely chopped

Equipment
25 x 38cm shallow baking tin

This is a wonderful dessert — it looks impressive and tastes really sophisticated but it is pretty simple to make. I love the praline flavour created by the combination of sweet meringue and hazelnuts.

Heat your oven to 180°C/gas 4 and line a 25 x 38cm shallow baking tin with baking parchment.

For the meringue, whisk the egg whites with an electric whisk or using a mixer with a whisk attachment, until they form firm peaks. Now whisk in half the sugar, a spoonful at a time, whisking well between each addition to make sure the sugar is fully incorporated. Lightly fold in the remaining sugar to make a stiff, glossy meringue.

Spread the meringue evenly in the prepared tin and sprinkle over the chopped hazelnuts. Bake for 15–20 minutes until risen, lightly golden and set. Have ready a large piece of baking parchment.

Carefully invert the meringue onto the paper, nut side down. Peel away the lining paper and leave to cool completely.

For the filling, whip the cream until it holds soft peaks. Beat the chocolate spread in another bowl until it is soft and fold it lightly into the whipped cream.

Spread the chocolate cream on top of the cooled meringue, leaving a 1cm margin at each edge. Sprinkle the grated chocolate over the cream, followed by the chopped hazelnuts.

Using a palette knife, make an indentation across the width of the meringue, about 1.5cm in from one of the short ends (this makes it easier to start rolling). Now, using the greaseproof paper to help you, roll up the roulade from that short end. Don't worry if it cracks a little – that's all part of its charm.

Carefully transfer the roulade to a rectangular serving plate or board and serve straight away.

Step photographs overleaf

Hazelnut meringue roulade

Spreading the stiff, glossy meringue in the prepared baking tin.

Sprinkling the chopped toasted hazelnuts evenly over the surface of the meringue.

Inverting the cooked meringue onto greaseproof paper and peeling away the lining paper.

Spreading the chocolate cream on top of the cooled meringue.

Making an indentation across the width of the meringue, about 1.5cm in from one edge.

Starting to roll up the meringue from the indented edge, using the greaseproof paper.

Continuing to roll up the roulade firmly and evenly, using the paper to help.

Removing the paper, ready to transfer the roulade to a serving plate or board.

Black Forest trifle

For the cherry blondies

225g unsalted butter,
cut into cubes

225g white chocolate, broken
into small pieces

225g caster sugar

4 medium eggs

½ tsp vanilla extract

175g self-raising flour

100g dark chocolate, chopped

100g glacé cherries, halved

For the chocolate custard

150ml double cream

150ml whole milk

4 medium egg yolks

100g caster sugar

30g plain flour

100g dark chocolate,
finely chopped

To assemble

3 tbsp Kirsch

2 x 470g jars morello cherries
in syrup, drained

1 x 340g jar cherry conserve
or jam

200g mascarpone

200ml double cream

To finish

25g dark chocolate, grated

Dark chocolate curls, pared
with a veg peeler (optional)

Equipment

20 x 26cm brownie tin

Large trifle bowl

Black Forest gâteau, with its blend of chocolate, cream, cherries and Kirsch, is a seventies classic that is still universally popular. This trifle uses the same combination of flavours to even more spectacular effect. If you don't have time to make the cherry blondies, buy a good ready-made sponge for the base instead.

Begin by making the blondies. Preheat your oven to 180°C/gas 4 and line a 20 x 26cm brownie tin with parchment.

Melt the butter and white chocolate together in a bowl over a pan of barely simmering water, stirring once or twice. Let cool slightly.

Whisk the sugar, eggs and vanilla together in a large bowl with an electric whisk or using a mixer for several minutes until pale, mousse-like and increased in volume. Slowly pour the melted chocolate mixture onto the eggs and fold in gently.

Add the flour and fold in lightly, then fold in the chopped dark chocolate. Pour into the lined tin and scatter over the glacé cherries.

Bake for about 30 minutes or until a skewer inserted into the centre comes out almost clean. Leave to cool in the tin.

To make the custard, put the cream and milk in a pan and heat until almost boiling. Take off the heat. Whisk the egg yolks, sugar and flour together, then pour on the hot milk and cream, whisking as you do so. Pour back into the pan and add the chocolate. Stir over a low heat until the chocolate has melted and the custard is well thickened. Strain into a jug and cover the surface of the custard with cling film (to prevent a skin forming). Leave to cool completely.

To assemble the trifle, cut about a third of the blondies into 2–3cm cubes and use to line the base of a large trifle bowl. (You won't need the rest here, but they will keep in an airtight tin for several days or you could use them for my chocolate bread and butter pudding on page 162.) Trickle over the Kirsch, so it soaks into the blondies. Scatter over the drained cherries, then spread over the cherry jam.

Spoon the cooled chocolate custard over the cherries then put into the fridge for several hours to allow the custard to set.

Whip the mascarpone with the cream until holding soft peaks, then swirl over the custard. Sprinkle with grated chocolate and decorate with chocolate curls, if using.

Cranachan cheesecake

SERVES 8

●●●●●●●○

For the base
125g unsalted butter, melted, plus extra for greasing

250g fine-milled oatcakes

3 tbsp honey

For the filling
60g pinhead (coarse) oatmeal

100g caster sugar

350g crowdie or ricotta

350g full-fat cream cheese

4 medium eggs

200g raspberries

For the raspberry coulis
500g raspberries

50g icing sugar

To finish
Handful of raspberries

Equipment
Deep 23cm springform cake tin

The classic Scottish dessert cranachan is a delicious blend of toasted oatmeal, raspberries, honey and crowdie – a type of soft, mild cheese. I've used those ingredients as the inspiration for this gorgeous cheesecake – make it in summer or early autumn when British raspberries are at their best. If you can't get hold of any crowdie, ricotta works equally well.

Butter a deep 23cm springform cake tin.

To make the base, put the oatcakes in a food processor and blitz until finely ground. Add the melted butter and honey and process briefly again until thoroughly combined. Press this mixture evenly into the base of the prepared tin. Chill in the fridge to set while you make the filling.

Heat your oven to 180°C/gas 4.

Heat a small frying pan over a medium heat. Add the oatmeal and 1 tsp of the sugar and toast, tossing frequently, until golden. Tip onto a plate to cool.

Put the crowdie or ricotta, cream cheese, eggs and remaining sugar in a food processor and blend until smooth. Stir in the cooled toasted oatmeal. Pour the mixture over the chilled oat base and scatter over the raspberries.

Bake for 35–40 minutes or until the cheesecake is set around the edges but still a bit wobbly in the middle. Turn off the oven and leave the cheesecake inside with the door ajar until it is cool. (Allowing it to cool slowly this way helps prevent it from cracking.)

Meanwhile, to make the raspberry coulis, purée the raspberries and icing sugar together in a blender, or using a handheld stick blender. Push the purée through a sieve into a jug to remove the pips.

Carefully unmould the cheesecake onto a large plate or board and cut into slices. Serve with fresh berries and the raspberry coulis.

Arctic roll

SERVES 8

●●●●●●●●

For the Swiss roll

A little sunflower oil for oiling

3 medium eggs

100g caster sugar, plus extra
for dusting

100g self-raising flour

1 tbsp warm water

For the filling

500ml good-quality vanilla
ice cream

200g raspberry jam

Equipment

22 x 32cm Swiss roll tin

This wonderfully retro pud dates back to the 1950s and is a fun way to round off a dinner party. Serve it just as it is or with fresh raspberries or strawberries on the side.

Heat your oven to 200°C/gas 6 and line a Swiss roll tin, 22 x 32cm or thereabouts, with baking parchment, and oil this very lightly.

For the filling, put the ice cream in a large bowl and beat it with the end of a rolling pin or something similar until just soft enough to mould. Scoop it onto a sheet of baking parchment and quickly shape into a sausage, 25–30cm long and about 5cm in diameter. Wrap in the parchment and place in the freezer to firm up.

To make the Swiss roll, use an electric whisk or a mixer with a whisk attachment to whisk the eggs and sugar together for several minutes until pale, moussey and almost tripled in volume. The mixture should be thick enough to hold a trail on the surface when the whisk is lifted. Sift the flour over the mixture and fold it in carefully. Fold in the warm water.

Pour the mixture into the prepared tin and smooth it out gently so it reaches into the corners. Bake for 10–12 minutes until golden and just firm to the touch.

Cut a sheet of baking parchment slightly larger than the Swiss roll tin, lay it on your work surface and sprinkle with sugar. Invert the cooked sponge onto the parchment and carefully peel away the lining paper from the sponge. Leave to cool completely.

To assemble the roll, first trim the two long sides of the sponge into neat, straight lines. Spread the jam over the sponge, leaving a 2cm margin along the edges.

Unwrap the ice cream and place it lengthways across the sponge, close to one edge. Use the parchment to help you roll the sponge around the ice cream. Use a bread knife to neatly trim each end of the roll.

Place the Arctic roll on a plate and serve straight away, cut into thick slices. You can wrap any of the roll that isn't eaten and return it to the freezer. Take it out and let it stand for a few minutes so the sponge can soften slightly, before slicing to serve.

Step photographs overleaf

Arctic roll

Shaping the ice cream into a roll in baking parchment and twisting the ends to secure.

Whisking the eggs and sugar together until the mixture is pale and thick enough to leave a trail.

Folding the flour into the whisked mixture, using a cutting and folding action.

Pouring the sponge mixture into the prepared Swiss roll tin.

Peeling the lining paper away from the sponge.

Positioning the frozen ice cream roll on the jam-topped sponge.

Rolling the sponge around the ice cream to enclose it.

Trimming off the ends of the Arctic roll.

Strawberry mousse cake

SERVES 8
●●●●●●●●

For the genoise sponge base
15g unsalted butter, melted,
plus extra for greasing
2 medium eggs
50g caster sugar
50g plain flour, sifted

For the mousse layer
135g packet strawberry jelly
1 tbsp water
200g strawberries
2 x 170g cans evaporated milk
250g strawberries, hulled and
cut in half top-to-toe (or sliced
into 3 if large)

To finish
50g dark chocolate, chopped
50g white chocolate, chopped
6–8 strawberries, hulled

Equipment
23cm springform cake tin
2 small greaseproof paper
piping bags

This is a really pretty gâteau, perfect to serve as a dessert for a summer party or special meal.

First make the sponge. Heat your oven to 180°C/gas 4. Butter and base-line a 23cm springform cake tin.

Put the eggs and sugar in a heatproof bowl over a pan of simmering water and whisk together using a handheld electric whisk until thick, pale and moussey, and doubled in volume. The mixture should hold a trail on the surface when you lift the whisk. Take off the heat and gently fold in the melted butter, then the flour.

Pour the mixture into the prepared tin and bake for 15–20 minutes until cooked and lightly golden. Leave to cool completely, then remove the sponge from the tin and peel off the paper.

Line the sides of the same tin with baking parchment, first snipping a line of parallel cuts along the base of the paper so it will fit snugly against the base. Put the sponge base back into the tin.

To make the mousse, break up the jelly and put it into a small pan with the water. Melt gently over a low heat until smooth. Take off the heat and set aside. Purée the 200g strawberries in a blender until smooth and pass through a sieve to remove the seeds.

Using an electric whisk or a mixer with a whisk attachment, whisk the evaporated milk for at least 5 minutes until it is thick, bubbly and doubled in volume. Gently fold in the liquid jelly, then fold in the strawberry purée.

Arrange the strawberry slices around the edge of the lined tin, cut side against the tin. Scatter any extra strawberries over the sponge. Pour the strawberry mousse into the tin and gently level the surface. It doesn't matter if the mousse doesn't quite cover the strawberries. Place in the fridge for at least 2 hours to set.

Carefully unmould the mousse cake onto a plate. To finish, melt the dark and white chocolate separately in bowls over hot water. Dip the strawberries into the melted dark chocolate to coat and place on parchment to set. Put the rest of the dark chocolate and the white chocolate into separate greaseproof paper piping bags, snip off the tip and drizzle lines of dark and white chocolate over the top of the mousse. Top with the chocolate-dipped strawberries and serve.

Step photographs overleaf

Strawberry mousse cake

Spooning the genoise mixture into the prepared springform tin.

Peeling away the lining paper from the base of the cooked sponge.

Fitting the cooled sponge into the base of the re-lined tin.

Adding the liquid jelly to the whisked evaporated milk.

Adding the strawberry purée to the evaporated milk and jelly mixture.

Positioning the strawberry slices around the edge of the cake tin, cut side outwards.

Carefully pouring the strawberry mousse mixture into the tin.

Drizzling melted chocolate decoratively over the surface of the set mousse.

Marmalade & almond cake

SERVES 8
●●●●●●●●

200g unsalted butter, softened, plus extra for greasing

150g semolina

75g ground almonds

½ tsp baking powder

200g caster sugar

3 tbsp fine-cut marmalade

2 medium eggs

Finely grated zest of 2 oranges

50ml orange juice

For the cream cheese frosting

175g cream cheese

25g unsalted butter, softened

100g icing sugar

To finish

Finely pared orange zest

Equipment

20cm springform cake tin

This is based on a classic orange polenta cake, though I prefer to use semolina rather than polenta, which can lead to a slight grittiness. Semolina gives the cake a lovely, fine texture but you can opt for polenta or fine cornmeal instead if you'd like to keep the cake wheat-free.

Heat your oven to 180°C/gas 4. Grease a 20cm springform cake tin with butter and line the base with baking parchment.

Combine the semolina, ground almonds and baking powder in a bowl, mix thoroughly and set aside.

Beat the butter and sugar together in a large bowl until pale and fluffy. Beat in the marmalade, then beat in the eggs, one at a time.

Add the semolina and almond mixture, along with the orange zest, and fold in gently. Finally, incorporate the orange juice to give a soft dropping consistency.

Spoon the mixture into the prepared cake tin and gently smooth the surface with the back of a spoon.

Bake for 35 minutes, or until the cake is golden brown. Leave in the tin to cool for 5 minutes, then remove and transfer to a wire rack to cool completely.

To make the frosting, beat the cream cheese and butter together. Sift in the icing sugar and beat until smooth. Use a palette knife to spread the frosting on top of the cake. Chill before serving, to allow the frosting to set.

Before serving, scatter fine shreds of orange zest on top of the cake for a decorative finish.

Lemon & lavender loaf

SERVES 8
●●●●●●●●

For the cake
250g plain flour
½ tsp baking powder
½ tsp bicarbonate of soda
125g caster sugar
1½ tbsp lavender (fresh buds
and leaves or edible dried
lavender)
Finely grated zest of 2 lemons
2 large eggs
200g full-fat plain yoghurt
100g unsalted butter, melted

For the lemon drizzle
Juice of 2 lemons, strained
2 tbsp icing sugar

For the topping
1 tbsp granulated sugar
2 tsp edible dried lavender

Equipment
1kg loaf tin, about 10 x 20cm
base measurement

This simple variation on the classic lemon drizzle works a treat. It has a wonderful, light texture, a very fresh taste and it looks incredibly pretty – perfect with a cuppa on a sunny afternoon. For advice on sourcing edible lavender, see page 187.

Heat your oven to 180°C/gas 4. Line a 1kg loaf tin (about 10 x 20cm base measurement) with baking parchment.

In a bowl, combine the flour, baking powder, bicarbonate of soda, sugar, lavender and lemon zest.

In a jug, beat the eggs with the yoghurt and melted butter until evenly blended. Pour this onto the dry ingredients and, using a spatula, stir until just combined.

Pour the mixture into the prepared tin and bake for 40 minutes or until a skewer inserted into the centre of the cake comes out clean.

Just before the cake is cooked, mix the ingredients for the drizzle together. Remove the cake from the oven and prick it deeply all over with a cocktail stick. Pour the lemon drizzle over the hot cake, then sprinkle over the granulated sugar followed by the lavender. Leave to cool completely in the tin before slicing.

Come-again cake

SERVES 8–10
● ● ● ● ● ● ● ● ● ●

200g unsalted butter, softened
150g caster sugar
200g self-raising flour
2 tbsp cocoa powder
2 medium eggs, beaten
2 tbsp golden syrup
200g mixed dried fruit
Finely grated zest and juice
of ½ lemon

Equipment
1kg loaf tin, about 10 x 20cm
base measurement

This lovely, fruity, lightly chocolatey cake is based on an old Yorkshire recipe. Its texture improves on keeping, hence the name. It will keep for up to a month, and is very good used in my chocolate bread and butter pudding (page 162).

Heat your oven to 160°C/gas 3. Line a 1kg loaf tin (about 10 x 20cm base measurement) with baking parchment.

Beat the butter and sugar together in a large bowl until pale and fluffy. Beat in 3 tbsp of the flour together with the cocoa powder, then gradually beat in the eggs. Fold in the remaining flour, then add the remaining ingredients and fold these in too.

Spread the mixture in the prepared tin and bake for 1½ hours or until a skewer inserted into the centre comes out clean. Leave to cool in the tin for 10 minutes, then turn out and cool on a rack. Store in an airtight tin.

Salted caramel & coffee éclairs

MAKES 8

●●●●●●●●

For the choux pastry

50g unsalted butter, cut into
roughly 1cm dice

1 tsp caster sugar

Pinch of salt

150ml water

65g strong white bread flour

2 medium eggs, beaten

For the coffee filling

200g mascarpone

1 tbsp icing sugar

3 tbsp cold strong coffee
(espresso is ideal)

250ml double cream

For the salted caramel icing

150g soft light brown sugar

75g unsalted butter, softened

Pinch of salt

50ml whole milk

125g icing sugar

Equipment

2 baking trays

Piping bag

1cm plain nozzle

If you think you couldn't turn out a batch of professional-looking and utterly irresistible éclairs, think again. These are very straightforward and will impress family and friends.

Heat your oven to 190°C/gas 5. Line two baking trays with baking parchment.

To make the choux pastry, put the butter, sugar, salt and water into a large saucepan. Heat gently until the butter has melted then bring to the boil. Immediately remove from the heat and tip in the flour. Beat with a wooden spoon to form a smooth ball of dough that leaves the sides of the pan.

Now vigorously beat the egg into the hot dough, a little at a time. This takes some elbow grease! As you add the egg, the dough will become stiff and glossy. Stop adding the egg if the dough starts to become loose – but you should use up all or most of it.

Spoon the choux paste into a piping bag fitted with a 1cm plain nozzle. Pipe eight 12cm lengths onto the baking trays, leaving plenty of space for spreading. Bake for 30 minutes, or until well risen and golden. Remove from the oven and split one side of each éclair to allow the steam to escape. Cool on a wire rack.

To make the filling, beat the mascarpone until smooth. Beat in the icing sugar and coffee. Whip the cream until it holds soft peaks and fold in. Spoon the mixture into a piping bag fitted with a 1cm plain nozzle and pipe into the éclairs.

To make the icing, put the sugar, butter and salt into a small pan and heat gently until the butter has melted and the mixture is smooth. Add the milk, bring to the boil and boil for 2 minutes, stirring occasionally. Remove from the heat and sift in the icing sugar. Stir until smooth.

Spread the icing on top of the éclairs. You'll need to work quickly before the icing sets but it can be reheated if it sets before you have finished. Serve the éclairs as soon as the icing is set.

Step photographs overleaf

Salted caramel & coffee éclairs

Spooning the choux paste into a piping bag.

Piping the choux paste into 12cm lengths on the lined baking trays.

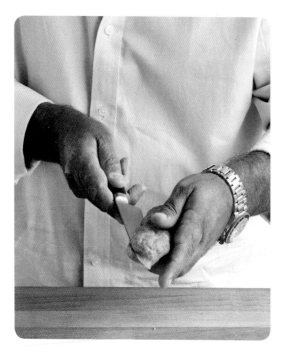

Splitting each cooked éclair along one side to release the steam from inside.

Piping the coffee filling into each éclair.

Spreading the salted caramel icing on top
of each éclair with a small palette knife.

Shortbread whisky dodgers

MAKES 12
●●●●●●●●●

For the biscuits
225g unsalted butter, softened

100g caster sugar, plus extra
for sprinkling

225g plain flour

100g fine semolina

For the whisky and white chocolate ganache
200g white chocolate,
broken into small pieces

100ml double cream

1½ tbsp whisky

Equipment
7.5cm cutter, plus small heart-
and/or star-shaped cutters

2 baking sheets

These are, of course, a sophisticated and delicious version of the classic jam-sandwich biscuit.

Beat the butter and sugar together in a large bowl until light and fluffy. Combine the flour and semolina, add to the butter mix and use a wooden spoon to start working in. When the mixture starts to form clumps, use your hands to bring it together into a smooth dough. Form it into a rough disc, wrap in cling film and chill for about an hour.

Heat your oven 170°C/gas 3. Line two baking sheets with baking parchment.

Tip the chilled dough onto a floured work surface and roll it out until about 3mm thick. Don't worry if it seems a little crumbly at first, just press it back together and re-roll.

Use a 7.5cm round cutter to cut out 24 discs of dough. Put these on the lined baking trays. Use a small star- and/or heart-shaped cutter to cut out shapes from the centre of half the discs.

Bake for 15 minutes, until the shortbread biscuits are just starting to turn golden at the edges. While still hot, sprinkle caster sugar over the biscuits with shapes cut out. Leave the biscuits on the trays to cool and firm up.

Meanwhile, to make the ganache filling, put the chocolate and double cream in a bowl. Heat over a pan of simmering water until the chocolate has melted, stirring from time to time to amalgamate the mixture. When completely smooth, stir in the whisky. Leave to cool, then cover and refrigerate for 2–3 hours, until firm.

To assemble the dodgers, spoon some ganache into the centre of each base biscuit (those that do not have shapes cut out) in a roughly circular shape, leaving a small gap around the edge. Alternatively, you can pipe the ganache onto the biscuits.

Sit the star or heart cut-out biscuits on top of the filling and press down very lightly. Repeat until all of the biscuits are sandwiched together. Serve as soon as they are assembled, as the biscuits will start to lose their crispness after a few hours.

Step photographs overleaf

Shortbread whisky dodgers

Stamping out discs of shortbread dough with a 7.5cm plain cutter.

Cutting out hearts or stars from the centre of half of the shortbread rounds.

Carefully lifting out the hearts and stars (these can be re-rolled to cut more biscuits).

Spreading the whisky and white chocolate ganache on the plain shortbread rounds.

Applying the star and heart cut-out biscuits
to sandwich the filling.

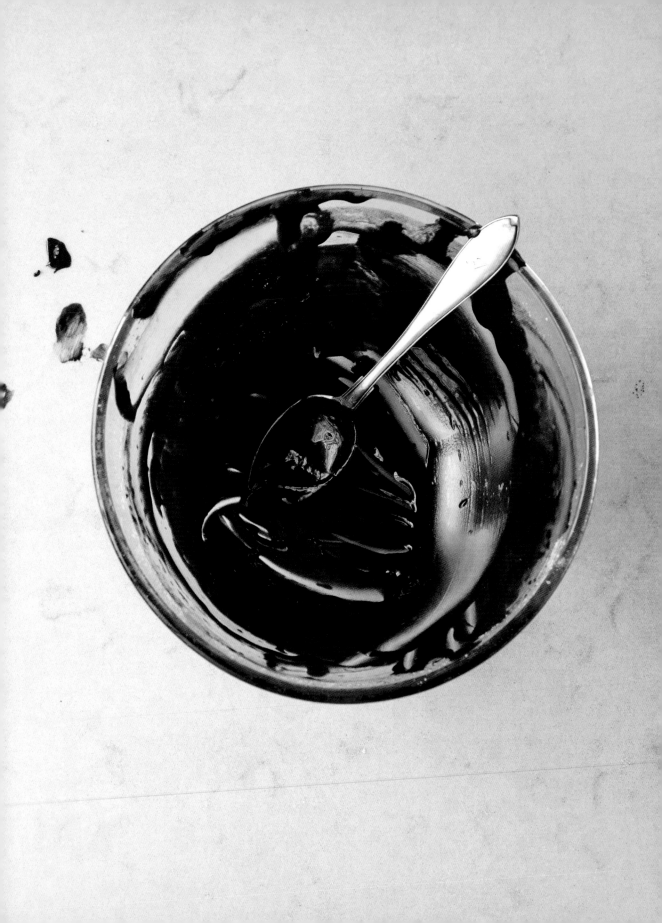

INDEX

To Josh – my special boy

Acknowledgments

Thank you to everybody involved in this book at Bloomsbury, in particular my editor Natalie Hunt, for her unstinting dedication to the project; Nikki Duffy and Janet Illsley, for their excellent work on the text; Jude Drake, Ellen Williams, Amanda Shipp, Roísín Nield, Nikki Morgan, Marina Asenjo and Xa Shaw Stewart for their support and creativity.

This book would not have been possible without the talents and patience of the wonderful Claire Bassano and the creative vision of photographer Peter Cassidy, and designers Peter Dawson and Louise Evans.

Thank you to the production team behind the series at Spun Gold Television, Nick Bullen, Chris Kelly and Dunk Barnes, and to Gerard Melling and Damian Kavanagh at the BBC for making it happen.

Finally thanks to my agents Geraldine Woods and Anna Bruce who championed this from the outset... and have always had a soft spot for pies and puds!

First published in Great Britain 2013

Text © Paul Hollywood 2013
Photography © Peter Cassidy 2013

By arrangement with the BBC. The BBC is a trademark of the British Broadcasting Corporation and is used under licence. BBC logo © BBC 1996.

The moral right of the author has been asserted.

Bloomsbury Publishing Plc, 50 Bedford Square, London WC1B 3DP
Bloomsbury Publishing, London, New Delhi, New York and Sydney
www.bloomsbury.com

A CIP catalogue record for this book is available from the British Library.
ISBN 978 1 4088 4643 8
10 9 8 7 6 5 4 3 2 1

Project editor: Janet Illsley
Designers: Peter Dawson, Louise Evans www.gradedesign.com
Photographer: Peter Cassidy
Food editor: Nikki Duffy
Recipe development consultant: Claire Bassano
Food stylists: Claire Bassano and Nikki Morgan
Props stylist: Roísín Nield
Indexer: Hilary Bird

Printed and bound by Mohn Media, Germany

MIX
Paper from responsible sources
FSC® C011124
www.fsc.org

Innovative use of combined heat and power technology when printing this product reduced CO_2 emissions by up to 52% in comparison to conventional methods in Germany.

minus 52% CO_2